Critical Essays on Hip Hop and the Study of Hip Hop

P. Khalil Saucier
Editor

Critical Essays on Hip Hop and the Study of Hip Hop

Doing the Knowledge

Editor
P. Khalil Saucier
Department of Critical Black Studies
Bucknell University
Lewisburg, PA, USA

ISBN 978-3-031-80762-6   ISBN 978-3-031-80763-3   (eBook)
https://doi.org/10.1007/978-3-031-80763-3

Pattern © John Rawsterne/patternhead.com

This Palgrave Macmillan imprint is published by the registered company Springer Nature Switzerland AG.
The registered company address is: Gewerbestrasse 11, 6330 Cham, Switzerland

If disposing of this product, please recycle the paper.

ACKNOWLEDGMENTS

Thanks to each of the contributors who stood beside me over the years as this project hit various and numerous political and intellectual barricades. Each contributor trusted that the project would eventually see print. I appreciate the indulgence of Palgrave Macmillan and thank you to the anonymous reviewer. Thanks to all the editors involved, especially Robin James for believing in the project from the jump.

CONTENTS

NOTES ON CONTRIBUTORS

Kevin P. Eubanks received his PhD in Comparative Literature from the University of North Carolina, Chapel Hill, USA, and is Associate Professor of Writing and Humanities at the U.S. Naval War College, Newport, RI, USA. His research interests and areas of expertise include critical theory and comparative literary and philosophical modernism(s).

M. Shadee Malaklou is Founder and Inaugural Director of the bell hooks center; Chair and Associate Professor of Women's, Gender, and Sexuality Studies at Berea College; and visiting faculty at Concordia University's Centre for Expanded Poetics. Malaklou's antiracist feminist interventions have been published in academic journals like *Theory & Event, Black Camera, Rhizomes, National Political Science Review, Journal for Critical Animal Studies*, and the *Journal of French and Francophone Philosophy*; and as public scholarship, in magazines like *Syndicate, CounterPunch, The Feminist Wire*, and *The Conversationalist*.

P. Khalil Saucier is Professor of Critical Black Studies at Bucknell University, USA. He is the author of *Necessarily Black: Cape Verdean Youth, Hip Hop Culture, and a Critique of Identity* (Michigan State Press, 2015) and co-author (with Tryon P. Woods) of *African Migrants, European Borders, and the Problem with Humanitarianism* (Lexington Books, 2024). He is also the editor and co-editor of various books, as well as co-editor of the book series Understanding Marronage: Critical and Cross-Disciplinary Engagements (Lexington Books).

Tryon P. Woods is Professor of Crime & Justice Studies at the University of Massachusetts, Dartmouth, USA. He is the author of *Blackhood Against the Police Power: Punishment and Disavowal in the "Post-Racial" Era* (Michigan State University Press, 2019); *Pandemic Police Power, Public Health, and the Abolition Question* (Palgrave Macmillan, 2022); *African Migrants, European Borders, and the Problem with Humanitarianism* (with P. Khalil Saucier) (Lexington Books, 2024); and *The Cinema of Social Death: Blackhood At-Large* (Rowman & Littlefield forthcoming).

Wind Dell Woods is a playwright, educator, and scholar. His creative and scholarly work explores, what he calls, disaesthetics in contemporary theater and performance. As a scholar, he disrupts the traditional tendency to freeze Hip Hop as an object of study. Rather, he reemploys Hip Hop as a method of study, a Black study, with the capacity to layer, sample, and (re)mix theories and analyses into a meta-critical cypher. His creative work centers on community, identity, death and rebirth, blackness, and performativity. He is Associate Professor of Theatre Arts at the University of Puget Sound, USA.

"Doing the Knowledge": A Critical Introduction

P. Khalil Saucier

The year that I entered graduate school to pursue a postgraduate degree was the same year that I decided that the study of hip hop would be central to any and all my academic endeavors henceforth. Serendipitously, soon after my intellectual pledge to self, I met several scholars on campus who were also interested in harnessing the intellectual and cultural energy of hip hop in order to better make sense of our world. We gathered to test the waters and gauge student interest in studying all the elements of hip hop culture. We called ourselves the Hip Hop Studies Collective and we organized lectures by practitioners and scholars, screened films, and more. Student and community interest was real, robust, and infectious. Our initial success led some Collective members, including myself, to envision a degree in hip hop studies, an audacious claim, for sure. In fact, before one of our film screenings and discussions, I announced that it was the Collective's intention to push the boundaries of the academy and establish a hip hop studies minor.

Yet, before we made any headway on establishing hip hop studies as a degree granting program, I had already started envisioning a course on

P. K. Saucier (✉)
Department of Critical Black Studies, Bucknell University, Lewisburg, PA, USA
e-mail: pks008@bucknell.edu

© The Author(s), under exclusive license to Springer Nature Switzerland AG 2025
P. K. Saucier (ed.), *Critical Essays on Hip Hop and the Study of Hip Hop*, https://doi.org/10.1007/978-3-031-80763-3_1

1

hip hop and in 2004 as a graduate student I introduced my 'sociology of hip hop' course to the campus community. On the first day of class, and to a full classroom of excited students to boot, I opened with a soliloquy on the importance of hip hop culture for studying patterns of social relationships, social interaction, and aspects of culture associated with everyday life. More so, I argued that hip hop culture opens up new vistas to examine how race, class, and gender intersect and impact all our lived experiences. In a nutshell, while I dramatized the promises of this new field of inquiry, I was fully committed to its promises and potentiality. Our course readings included a good mix of popular and journalistic accounts on hip hop, classic texts, namely the ur-text of hip hop studies *Black Noise* by Tricia Rose, and seminal works such as Mark Anthony Neil and Murray Forman's encyclopedic work *That's the Joint: The Hip Hop Studies Reader.*[1] Using a black cultural studies frame, in particular the work of Paul Gilroy and Stuart Hall, we constructed a valuable prism of critique, testament, theory, and contestation.[2]

At the end of fifteen weeks, 65 students and I did something historic and intellectually productive which led me to teach the class a few more times before I graduated and took a tenure-track job.[3] Fast forward over 20 years, anthropology, art history, literature, religious studies, and sociology courses on hip hop classes are beyond fashionable, while majors, minors, and graduate certifications in hip hop studies have become slowly more available.[4] In a sense, the Collective's dream about hip hop having a larger stake in the academy has become a reality, for hip hop is now a constitutive element of the modern academy both locally and globally. In addition to degrees and courses, the level of scholarly production has proliferated with conferences, book series, and journals dedicated strictly

[1] Tricia Rose, *Black noise: Rap music and Black cultural resistance in contemporary American popular culture* (Middletown: Wesleyan University, 1994); Murray Forman and Mark Anthony Neal, eds., *That's the joint!: the hip-hop studies reader* (New York: Routledge, 2004).

[2] One could argue that the mode of inquiry in early iterations of hip hop studies was simply a sub-field of black cultural studies.

[3] In 2002 said class was awarded the best class to take in the Boston area by the high-circulating *Metro Boston*, the free daily newspaper, a class that trumped even those taught by Cornel West and others in the surrounding proximity.

[4] For example, the University of Arizona, Bowie State University, Howard University, Loyola University-New Orleans, Columbia College-Chicago, and North Carolina Central University all have majors and minors in hip hop studies, while the University of Colorado-Boulder offers a graduate concentration in hip hop studies.

to the study of hip hop.[5] In fact, not only was I teaching courses attentive to hip hop culture, I too was presenting papers at conferences and writing about hip hop, in particular its relationship to blackness.[6]

As the study of hip hop expanded its theories, methods, and findings—broadening the objects and agents of its inquiry—my skepticism about the growth of this burgeoning field also began to develop. In addition to its expansion, the fetishization of the ways in which to study hip hop culture began to harden, leaving important aspects of the culture and what practitioners actually said about the social world by the wayside. In other words, what was developing was an idèe fixe for translating the subversive deconstruction of individualism within hip hop culture and nothing more.

For instance, as philosopher Jim Vernon has observed, "The aesthetic practices of Hip Hop have thus frequently been deployed to justify an ethics and/or politics focused on perpetual acts of *negation, refusal, opposition*, or *subversion*."[7] Furthermore, Vernon suggests that "Hip Hop Studies ... encourages scholars to 'sample' fragments of the history of the culture ... for ends isolated from, and often at odds with, the intentions of the culture's creators."[8] Too often it is the individual, the self that is prioritized, while the black community is mobilized only to make a point, producing what anthropologist João Costa Vargas calls "oblique identification." For Vargas, "oblique identification" is when "Black processes are recognized only partially, belatedly, indirectly, reluctantly, or even unknowingly."[9]

Taking my cue from philosopher Lewis R. Gordon and his observations about "disciplinary decadence," I started to practice the teleological suspension of hip hop studies.[10] Gordon suggests that "Disciplinary decadence

[5] See, for example, *Journal of Hip Hop Studies* and *Global Hip Hop* and the University of California Press's Hip Hop Studies Series and Routledge Studies in Hip Hop and Religion.

[6] See, for example, P. Khalil Saucier, *Necessarily Black: Cape Verdean youth, hip-hop culture, and a critique of identity* (East Lansing: Michigan State University Press, 2015a); P. Khalil Saucier, "Continental drift: the politics and poetics of African hip hop," in *Sounds and the City: Popular Music, Place, and Globalization.* 196–208, (London: Palgrave Macmillan UK, 2014); P. Khalil Saucier and Kumarini Silva, "Keeping it real in the global south: Hip-hop comes to Sri Lanka," *Critical Sociology* 40.2 (2014): 295–300.

[7] Jim Vernon, *Sampling, biting, and the postmodern subversion of hip hop* (Cham, Switzerland; Palgrave Macmillan, 2021), 2.

[8] Vernon, *Sampling, biting,* 28–29.

[9] João H. Costa Vargas, *The Denial of Antiblackness: Multiracial redemption and black suffering* (Minneapolis: University of Minnesota Press, 2018), 5.

[10] Lewis R. Gordon, *Disciplinary Decadence: Living thought in trying times* (New York: Routledge, 2015).

is when a discipline treats itself as reality, instead of something trying to have a *relationship* with reality. So, it ignores other disciplines, what others have to say—in other words, it becomes, in existential terms, *serious*."[11] Rather than "do the knowledge," hip hop studies became in a word too serious, closed off from what was actual.[12] The goal, I thought, was not simply to translate hip hop culture into narratives of refusal; rather find within hip hop culture, that is, its organic modes of critique and methodologies that reflect what philosopher William D. Hart calls "the discourse of blackness of black [which] explains relations among blackness, antiblackness, and Black people."[13] Or, as philosopher James Haile has cogently argued, something like Kendrick Lamar's album, *good kid, m.A.A.d city,* "offers a new way of thinking about hip-hop as a whole, not simply as a capitalistic enterprise or as a 'black news' channel, but as a distinct method for collecting data and understanding the experiences and existence of black people."[14]

As a result of my practice of suspension, along with my fidelity to black study as a transdisciplinary practice and hip hop culture, I co-authored an essay with scholar Tryon P. Woods, titled "Hip Hop Studies in Black" in 2016.[15] The essay offered a synergistic critique between hip hop studies and black studies in order to further understand the blackness that sits at the center of hip hop culture—hoping that hip hop studies would take seriously the culture's renegade ethos. Our conclusion was that much of what was called hip hop studies was not ethically accountable to blackness and black struggle, despite the dynamic blackness plays within the culture. In other words, our purpose was to set the record straight that hip hop

[11] Jack Madden, "Fear of Black Consciousness: Lewis Gordon Interview," *Philosophy Break*, Accessed June 15, 2024. https://philosophybreak.com/articles/fear-of-black-consciousness-lewis-gordon-interview/, n.p. emphasis in original. For more on the idea of seriousness, see Lewis R. Gordon, *Fear of Black consciousness* (London: Penguin UK, 2022).

[12] See, for example, Jim Vernon, *Hip Hop, Hegel, and the Art of Emancipation: Let's Get Free.* (Cham, Switzerland: Springer, 2018).

[13] William David Hart, *The Blackness of Black: Key Concepts in Critical Discourse* (Lanham, MD: Rowman & Littlefield, 2020), 231.

[14] James B. Haile III, "Good kid, mAAd city: Kendrick Lamar's autoethnographic method," *JSP: Journal of Speculative Philosophy* 32.3 (2018): 489.

[15] P. Khalil Saucier and Tryon P. Woods. "Hip hop studies in black," *Journal of Popular Music Studies* 26.2–3 (2014): 268–294. See also, P. Khalil Saucier and Tryon P. Woods. "Upgrade and Upstage: Injunctions Against Stephanie Rawlings-Blake, "Black Feminism," and Hip Hop Studies at the Ledge (A Response to Forster)," *Journal of Popular Music Studies* 27.3 (2015b): 353–363.

studies was superfluous and that the best versions of hip hop studies were black studies. Needless to say, the essay unnerved more than a few readers. In fact, the journal received a submission in response to our essay which objected to the structural analysis that we were advancing in place of an individual level of analysis. The journal agreed to publish said response, while giving us an opportunity to also respond, which they also published.[16] As authors attempting to make an intervention, we were excited that a critical dialogue was being constructed. Setting hubris aside, we honestly thought the essay, published in a popular music journal, could have some impact on the field's modes of inquiry, and most importantly its analyses. Yet, and unfortunately, after nearly a decade little has changed in hip hop studies.[17] In the most general sense, it seems as if it is stuck in place chasing the shadow of urban and now rural youth identity worldwide. Many hip hop studies scholars remain attached to racial identity, while black people globally confront antiblackness. If identity remains the sole focus, rather than the paradigmatic reality that structures the phenomenological and lived experience, then the result will inevitably be an overemphasis on identity politics and agentic subversion. To put it plainly, hip hop studies is often "tethered to the colonizer's speech," mindlessly upholding and inserting its highly problematic construction of hip hop as it relates to blackness and by extension failing its own by not taking seriously what Sylvia Wynters describes as the "monohumanism" structuring black life in the twenty-first century.[18]

Hip hop culture is most often understood as derivative of a myriad of global political and economic forces, the cultural progeny of racial capitalism, a product of a renewed capitalist class offensive and racialized strategies of social control in the US. As such, hip hop studies prioritizes the political economy and presupposes a "genre of the human" that is

---

[16] N. Forster, "What is This Thing Called Hip Hop Studies?: A Response to Saucier and Woods," *Journal of Popular Music Studies*, 27 (2015): 343–352.

[17] Although it should be noted that said essay was included in the latest edition of *That's the joint*. See Murray Forman, Mark Anthony Neal, and Regina N. Bradley eds., *That's the Joint: The Hip-Hop studies reader* (New York: Routledge. 2024).

[18] David Marriott, *Whither Fanon?: studies in the blackness of being* (Palo Alto: Stanford University Press, 2018), 90. See also, Greg Thomas, "Wynter with Fanon in the FLN: The" Rights of Peoples" against the" Monohumanism" of" Man"," *American Quarterly* 70.4 (2018): 857–865.

singular, yet composed of a kaleidoscope of colors and identities.[19] Hip hop studies envisions planet rock "as the transcendental plane of humanity,"[20] thus extending an epistemic vice that continues to be structural and paradigmatic, in turn failing to apprehend how racial blackness serves as the onto-epistemic anchor for "race" in all of its permutations. Confusing the structural for the empirical leads to an analysis of race (and resistance) that misses the essential violence of antiblackness and is grounded in an inaccurate understanding of racism. What appears heterogeneous at the level of lived experience and interpersonal relations fades to black, if you will, at the level of structural positionality. Despite spanning the political and sociological to the poetic and creative, the field says little about the materiality of violence that incarnates (non)beings. Race is part of any and all understanding of hip hop, for its residual effects can be found in all language, memory, and subjectivity. While there has been an increase in interest in processes of racialization within hip hop culture, whereby race is understood to be reproduced in the present, blackness becomes merely a historical referent and/or empirical supplement, rather than the source and sequence of modernity. In other words, any quick glance at many of the central texts within hip hop studies shows that race is central to their discourse, but only insofar as blackness is eventually displaced or understood only as a marker for cultural identity or identification.

While hip hop scholars are right to engage race within capitalist society, what goes missing is an awareness that blackness functions differently from "otherness," especially since "otherness" is not (non)being in the same way as blackness. Throughout this volume, blackness is understood to be a positionality, not an essentialized cultural identity or biological property. In deploying blackness strictly as a form of identity, hip hop studies constrains more radical forms of black struggle. To put it simply, the essays in this volume are not interested in phenomenological declarations of identity, if anything, these works highlight the problem at hand, that is, the ease with which radical examples of black struggle and movement are emptied of their radical content and translated into liberal

---

[19] See Sylvia Wynter and K. McKittrick, "Unparalleled catastrophe for our species? Or, to give humanness a different future: Conversations," in K. McKittrick, ed. *Sylvia Wynter: On being human as praxis*. 9–89. Durham: Duke University Press, 2015.

[20] Claire Colebrook, *Who Would You Kill to Save the World?*. (Lincoln: University of Nebraska Press, 2023), 77.

politics; individual agents of change and nothing more. Radical critique works beyond the pale of white non-black civil society, while much of what constitutes hip hop studies gestures toward a liberal reformist frame of thinking that works from within. The ideas and histories of blackness from the Bronx to Mumbai are used not for its own liberation, but as a way in which to recuperate a liberal pluralism that undergirds global hip hop studies. Rather than a critique of modernity and its condition of possibility in and through blackness, hip hop studies positions the culture in support of modernity. For instance, the error in this form of thinking is the problem of universality as envisioned by the catch-all "global hip hop," a universality that takes for granted the general contours of humanity and sociality. Whether explicit or not, the cognitive mechanisms of hip hop studies are rooted in liberal western monohumanism, which, according to many from within the black radical tradition such as Aimè Cèsaire, Sylvia Wynter, Lewis R. Gordon, and many more fail to understand that race contains an anthropological rubric for the human of which the anti-human is the yardstick.[21] In other words, the doxastic attitude within hip hop studies circles more generally assumes that antiblackness is merely consciousness and can be rejected by simply assuming one's humanity. The presupposition of granting humanity and sociality is not simply and merely a form of consciousness. According to Moon-Kie Jung and João Costa Vargas, such a presupposition "operates under the assumption that racism, or white supremacy, impacts all peoples of color in related (if distinct), commensurable (if incommensurate) ways and that our modern sociality and institutions are repairable, redeemable, perfectible."[22] This should not be read as a deterministic declaration, an absolute that renders transformation impossible, but as a more honest assessment of a historical condition. In doing so, the study of hip hop begins to look different, bucking prepackaged regimes of western knowledge that then engage "alternative genres of the human" as Sylvia Wynters has urged us to do.[23]

---

[21] See, for example, Aimè Cèsaire, *Discourse on colonialism* (New York: NYU Press, 2000); Lewis R. Gordon, *Existentia Africana: understanding Africana existential thought* (New York: Routledge, 2013); Sylvia Wynter, "Unsettling the coloniality of being/power/truth/freedom: Towards the human, after man, its overrepresentation—An argument," *CR: The new centennial review* 3.3 (2003): 257–337.

[22] Moon-Kie Jung, and João H. Costa Vargas, "More than and beyond racism: theoretical and political meditations on antiblackness," *Souls* 23.3–4 (2022): n.p.

[23] Wynter and McKitrick, "Unparalleled Catastrophe," 9–89.

Fundamentally, this volume asks a singular question, how do we rethink our approach to the study of hip hop in a way that does not reproduce the relations of power that so many scholars are attempting to unmask? Yet, much of hip hop scholarship is stuck in a call-and-response loop of certain forms of knowledge production that may in fact stifle liberation. That is, the essays in this volume help train our attention to the ways in which any and all presuppositions about blackness as merely a cultural-historical metaphor "utterly fails Black people."[24] In hip hop argot, "doing the knowledge" then asserts an active practice of exploration that echoes the unease of Dixa Ramirez-D'Oleo when she states that "of concern here is how black culture and sociality are weaponized to silence scholarship on anti-blackness."[25]

Given its theoretical and philosophical orientation, some readers may take this volume as: (1) a cynical and unwarranted collection of essays against a culture and a movement that has powerfully affected the world as we know it; and (2) a skeptical and under-theorized exposè on hip hop culture which fails to take seriously the idea of *hip hop as text* and in doing so stunting our understanding of black knowledge production more generally. Then again, *Critical Essays on Hip Hop and the Study of Hip Hop: Doing the Knowledge* is a movement in anticipation of a *blackened* next step in hip hop studies, given that each essay takes a deeper look into the utility of hip hop *for* and *of* thought itself; an expression of black thought, which is to say, an expression of black study that stands and thinks against the supremacy of the monohumanism of the west. Rather than confuse the empirical (e.g., the racial identity paradigm) for the structural, each chapter illustrates how the onto-epistemic structure of humanity and the social haunts how we understand hip hop culture and as a consequence limit the conditions of possibility that hip hop culture may present.

Additionally, others may think that the essays within this volume undermine the theoretical power of hip hop as text. While it is certainly true that hip hop has been under theorized, this volume is less interested in the ways in which hip hop can be seen as a theory and more so how scholars tend to theorize hip hop culture. In other words, this volume exposes the often unacknowledged ways that radical political movements and scholarship perpetuate antiblackness by concentrating and focusing on

---

[24] Jung, and Vargas. "More than and beyond racism," n.p.

[25] Dixa. Ramírez-D'Oleo, *This Will Not Be Generative* (Cambridge: Cambridge University Press, 2023), footnote 32, page 20.

experience, for instance, rather than existence. It shows how antiblackness positions bodies in very particular ways, no matter how the people in question act or define themselves (e.g., no matter how dope an emcee one is). In doing so, the volume helps problematize identity-based politics, as they relate to hip hop, that either neglect or flatten political ontology so that blackness is not simply reduced to a representable position (as expressed through hip hop). This is not to reduce the very real heterogeneity at the individual level (i.e., understanding the intimate connection between racial identity and hip hop), but rather better explicate for the reader blackness as the "position of the unthought."[26] This structure of antiblackness constitutes "the culture of politics" that begets global hip hop studies and by relying on the history of self-expression and subversive deconstructionism, does little to test the limits of an oppressive world.[27] The black studies tradition that the contributors draw from, notes that there is a culture that underwrites the very debates over representation that we almost exclusively recognize as "politics." This culture is not up for discussion; it is the taken-for-granted premise for all discourse. To make it plain, the purpose is to drill down into this level of culture, for engaging with *hip hop as text* and only text has left us with a theoretical vacuum. In short, this volume attempts to pull us away from the racial liberalism that reads every lyrical and visual refrain, for example, as a moment of liberation and freedom, and while a stimulus for generating the culture, antiblackness often remains a conceptual void for hip hop scholars.

As I limned, along with Tryon Woods, nearly a decade ago, "Hip hop studies will remain utterly wretched unless it comes to terms with the structure of gratuitous violence in which it exists. In order to chart an ethical future, hip hop studies, particularly those interested in blackness, must *become* black studies, and in so doing, confront the ways in which black existence in an antiblack world—in other words, a universe where black life is structurally impermissible—is bound up with [...] a fugitive

---

[26] Saidiya V. Hartman, and Frank B. Wilderson III, "The position of the unthought," *Qui Parle* 13.2 (2003): 183–201.

[27] For more on "the culture of politics," see Linette Park, "Afropessimism and Futures of...: A Conversation with Frank Wilderson," *The Black Scholar* 50.3 (2020): 29–41; Fernando Gomez Herrero and Frank B. Wilderson III, "The Afropessimist Never Drinks the Kool-Aid of Black Enlightened Progress: An Interview with Frank B. Wilderson III," *Diacritics* 50.4 (2022): 72–97; Frank B. Wilderson III, *Red, white & black: Cinema and the structure of US antagonisms* (Durham: Duke University Press, 2010).

life 'lived in loss.'"[28] In the end, *Critical Essays on Hip Hop and the Study of Hip Hop: Doing the Knowledge* is a collection that provides a much-needed perspective on hip hop and the study of hip-hop. It is an event of sorts: an interdisciplinary collection of debates and interventions by scholars and intellectuals in Black Studies, Cultural Studies, English, Gender Studies, and Education. The perspectives are theoretical and practical, philosophical and historical, engaging a variety of theories and practices. By reimagining important conversations with black studies, critical theory, and beyond it presents a way out of the multiple omissions characterizing hip hop studies, for hip hop studies generally does not elevate racial analysis to the privileged position that it accords to political economy, neoliberalism, identity, and more; and when racism is addressed, it is as an extension of the liberal conception of the social that continues to rely upon racial violence. Unlike most hip hop scholarship, however, *Critical Essays on Hip Hop and the Study of Hip Hop: Doing the Knowledge* is accountable to the socialization of racial slavery, and as such, is better equipped to confront the ontological and epistemological violence underwriting the modern world, and with hip hop studies more specifically. In the end, hip hop studies too often charts a course of investigation that is at odds with hip hop culture itself. Another way of exploring this is that hip hop scholars are forever transitioning between shadow and illumination. Yet, darkness itself is not the problem. As such, the real problem is not that hip hop studies pays too much attention to agency and racial capital. The problem is the blackness of hip hop culture only becomes black because of its object not for its optic and, as a consequence, hip hop studies is not black enough so as to commune with the darkness of the real. At the expense of ending on a trite note, hip hop studies, ironically, fears a blackened planet.

BIBLIOGRAPHY

Cèsaire, Aimè. *Discourse on Colonialism*. New York: NYU Press, 2000.
Colebrook, Claire. *Who Would You Kill to Save the World?*. Lincoln: University of Nebraska Press, 2023.
Forster, N. "What is This Thing Called Hip Hop Studies?: A Response to Saucier and Woods." *Journal of Popular Music Studies*, 27 (2015): 343-352.
Forman, Murray, and Mark Anthony Neal, eds. *That's the joint!: the hip-hop studies reader*. New York: Routledge, 2004.

---

[28] Saucier and Woods, "Hip Hop Studies in Black," 285.

Forman, Murray, Mark Anthony Neal, and Regina N. Bradley, eds., *That's the Joint: The Hip-Hop studies reader*, New York: Routledge. 2024.

Gordon, Lewis R. *Existentia Africana: understanding Africana existential thought*. New York: Routledge, 2013.

———. *Disciplinary Decadence: Living thought in trying times*. New York: Routledge, 2015.

———. *Fear of Black consciousness*. London: Penguin UK, 2022.

Haile III, James B. "Good kid, mAAd city: Kendrick Lamar's autoethnographic method." *JSP: Journal of Speculative Philosophy* 32, no. 3 (2018): 488-498.

Hart, William David. *The Blackness of Black: Key Concepts in Critical Discourse*. Lanham, MD: Rowman & Littlefield, 2020.

Hartman, Saidiya V., and Frank B. Wilderson III. "The position of the unthought." *Qui Parle* 13.2 (2003): 183-201.

Herrero, Fernando Gomez, and Frank B. Wilderson III. "The Afropessimist Never Drinks the Kool-Aid of Black Enlightened Progress: An Interview with Frank B. Wilderson III." *Diacritics* 50.4 (2022): 72-97.

Jung, Moon-Kie, and João H. Costa Vargas. "More than and beyond racism: theoretical and political meditations on antiblackness." *Souls* 23.3-4 (2022): n.p

Madden, Jack. "Fear of Black Consciousness: Lewis Gordon Interview." *Philosophy Break*, Accessed June 15, 2024. https://philosophybreak.com/articles/fear-of-black-consciousness-lewis-gordon-interview/, n.p.

Marriott, David. *Whither Fanon?: studies in the blackness of being*. Palo Alto: Stanford University Press, 2018.

Park, Linette. "Afropessimism and Futures of...: A Conversation with Frank Wilderson." *The Black Scholar* 50.3 (2020): 29-4.

Ramírez-D'Oleo, Dixa. *This Will Not Be Generative*. Cambridge: Cambridge University Press, 2023,

Rose, Tricia. *Black noise: Rap music and Black cultural resistance in contemporary American popular culture*. Middletown: Wesleyan University, 1994.

Saucier, P. Khalil, "Continental drift: the politics and poetics of African hip hop." In *Sounds and the City: Popular Music, Place, and Globalization*, 196-208. London: Palgrave Macmillan UK, 2014.

———. *Necessarily Black: Cape Verdean youth, hip-hop culture, and a critique of identity*. (East Lansing: Michigan State University Press, 2015a).

Saucier, P. Khalil, and Kumarini Silva. "Keeping it real in the global south: Hip-hop comes to Sri Lanka." *Critical Sociology* 40, no. 2 (2014): 295-300.

Saucier, P. Khalil, and Tryon P. Woods. "Hip hop studies in black." *Journal of Popular Music Studies* 26.2-3 (2014): 268-294.

Saucier, P. Khalil. "Upgrade and Upstage: Injunctions Against Stephanie Rawlings-Blake,"Black Feminism," and Hip Hop Studies at the Ledge (A Response to Forster)." *Journal of Popular Music Studies* 27.3 (2015b): 353-363.

Thomas, Greg. "Wynter with Fanon in the FLN: The "Rights of Peoples" against the "Monohumanism" of "Man"." *American Quarterly* 70.4 (2018): 857-865.

Vargas, João H Costa. *The Denial of Antiblackness: Multiracial redemption and black suffering*. Minneapolis: University of Minnesota Press, 2018.

Vernon, Jim. *Hip Hop, Hegel, and the Art of Emancipation: Let's Get Free*. Cham, Switzerland; Palgrave Macmillan, 2018.

———. *Sampling, biting, and the postmodern subversion of hip hop*. Cham, Switzerland; Palgrave Macmillan, 2021.

Wilderson III Frank B. *Red, white & black: Cinema and the structure of US antagonisms*. Durham: Duke University Press, 2010.

Wynter, Sylvia. "Unsettling the coloniality of being/power/truth/freedom: Towards the human, after man, its overrepresentation—An argument." *CR: The new centennial review* 3.3 (2003): 257-337.

Wynter, S., and K. McKittrick. "Unparalleled catastrophe for our species? Or, to give humanness a different future: Conversations." In K. McKittrick, ed. *Sylvia Wynter: On being human as praxis*. 9–89. Durham: Duke University Press, 2015.

"Peep the Technique": Afropessimism and Hip Hop's "Turn Toward Blackness"

Kevin P. Eubanks

In a world structured by the twin axioms of white superiority and black inferiority, of white existence and black nonexistence […]—in this world, the zero degree of transformation is the turn toward blackness […].[1]

Just as Frank Wilderson III cites the propensity of the black performance to obstruct rather than galvanize black political and social possibility, Jared Sexton questions Fred Moten's positive emphasis on the "fugitive being" of blackness that, according to Sexton, has blackness inevitably *on*

This chapter is a revised version of an article originally published as "After Blackness, Then Blackness: Afro-Pessimism, Black Life, and Classical Hip Hop as Counter-Performance" (*Journal of Hip-Hop Studies*, 4.1 [2017]).

[1] Jared Sexton, 2011.

K. P. Eubanks (✉)
U.S. Naval War College, Department of Writing and Humanities, Newport, RI, USA
e-mail: kevin.eubanks@usnc.edu

P. K. Saucier (ed.), *Critical Essays on Hip Hop and the Study of Hip Hop*, https://doi.org/10.1007/978-3-031-80763-3_2

13

the run from the structural impasse that governs its existence a priori.[2] According to Wilderson and Sexton, the core challenge of the afropessimist project is to imagine amidst the afropessimist negation a more vital black movement that is *not* or *other* than performative, something more than a "narrative strategy hoping to slip the noose of a life shaped by slavery."[3] Only in the wake of this more visceral confrontation with antiblackness can black art and culture convert the ghosts of slavery into what Wilderson calls "a grammar of emergence and being" that might then be capable of translation into a fully realized black political power and autonomy.[4]

In classical hip hop one can discern just such a three-fold movement. First, more than any other genre of black performance hip hop directly confronts the racist architecture of antiblackness in the sense called for by afropessimism. As a result of this confrontation, in what Jared Sexton describes as the "zero degree of transformation," blackness encounters itself in its unique predicament vis-à-vis this structural barrier to its existence.[5] On the other side of Sexton's "turn toward" itself or, better, *in* this turning, blackness conceives of itself anew in such a way that gives voice to another blackness altogether, one that poses a much more imminent threat to the integrity and survivability of the structural impasse insofar as it brings blackness one step closer to freedom and civil society one step closer to abolition.

HIP HOP AND AFROPESSIMISM

On his breakthrough 1996 album *Reasonable Doubt*, Jay-Z asks his listeners the essentially tragic question, "Can I live?" In doing so, he not only asks the same question that lies at the heart of the afropessimist tradition, but he also conjures to mind the history of hip hop's inquiry into the status and nature of black social life and the lived experience of so many in the black community: "We hustle out of a sense of hopelessness, sort of a desperation ... we feel we have nothing to lose, so we offer you, well, we

---

[2] Frank Wilderson, "Grammar and Ghosts: The Performative Limits of African Freedom," *Theatre Survey* 50, no. 1 (2009): 119–25; Jared Sexton, "The Social Life of Social Death: On Afro-Pessimism and Black Optimism," *InTensions* 5 (2011): 1–47; Fred Moten, "The Case of Blackness," *Criticism* 50, no. 2 (2008): 214.

[3] Wilderson, "Grammar and Ghosts," 122.

[4] Wilderson, "Grammar and Ghosts," 119.

[5] Sexton, "Social Life," 28–9.

offer our lives. What do you bring to the table?" In fact, with this despondent, but still defiant, refrain Jay-Z asks *the* question that echoes throughout slavery's afterlife and stages his own encounter with the problem of whether hip hop might somehow craft a free black existence out of social death; in the process, he reinforces the dominant leitmotif both of afropessimism and of hip hop in its classical era.[6]

On the one hand, classical hip hop's embrace of the *hustle*, the *game*, and all aspects of urban *street life* reflects the "outlaw" and "criminal" ontology upon which Fred Moten bases his "pre(optical) optimism" in "The Case of Blackness" and through which he locates an escape route to black independence.[7] The black "fugitive" subject is, in a sense, Moten suggests, free—free to create its lines of flight and, insofar as it is in flight, the figure of the fugitive remains not only permanently on the verge of realizing its escape but also remains in itself "the dislocation of black social life that [it] carries."[8] On the other hand, this figure lives just as permanently in fear and in danger of being apprehended (again), a dilemma afropessimism insists is not so easily overcome. Further, afropessimism's cautious apprehension surrounding the possibility of black social life, especially insofar as it is called a "fugitive" life, is equally in play across the hip hop aesthetic and an embedded feature of its political ontology, as tracks like Kool G Rap and DJ Polo's "On the Run" (1992), one of the genre's earliest and most obvious acknowledgments of this particular crisis of double-consciousness, unequivocally remind listeners. Poised against the positive value assigned to such performativity is the constant reminder that these signs of life are nevertheless only shadows of life, a distinctive impasse that situates hip hop's performance of blackness alongside the contemporary debate between black optimists and afropessimists, especially where that debate pivots on the limits of black performativity.

It thrusts us, for instance, into the orbit of Saidiya Hartman's seminal commentary in *Scenes of Subjection* on the simultaneous effects of the slave performance, where "[o]ne performance [is] aimed to reproduce and

---

[6] Also known as the Golden Age, the classical era of hip-hop extends from the mid-1980s to the mid-1990s, from the emergence of mainstream rap in figures such as Run-DMC, Erik B. and Rakim, and LL Cool J to the untimely deaths of Tupac Shakur and Notorious BIG in 1996 and 1997, respectively. See, for example, Ben Duinker and Denis Martin, "In Search of the Golden Age of Hip-Hip Sound (1986–1996)," *Empirical Musicology Review* 12.1–2 (2017): 80–100.
[7] Moten, "Case," 182.
[8] Moten, "Case," 211.

secure the relations of domination and the other to manipulate appearances in order to challenge these relations and create a space for action not generally available."[9] For Hartman, any modicum of free movement granted in the performance is simultaneously challenged, ontologically and structurally, by the circumstances of its expression: "Since acts of resistance exist within the context of relations of domination and are not external to them, they acquire their character from these relations, and vice-versa."[10] Conventional scholarship in hip hop studies generally comes down on one or the other side of Hartman's simultaneity. As in "On the Run," hip hop is said either to effectively undermine the status quo through various means, including criminal lines of flight, or, as a result of such criminality, to merely reproduce the terms of its captivity.[11]

Whereas Hartman's scene carves out "a space for action not generally available," Frank Wilderson's short but incisive critique in "Grammar and Ghosts" goes much further than Hartman's by denying altogether "any causal link between the performance and the emancipation of the black people who produced and consumed it—as though art was the very essence of, rather than an accompaniment to, structural change."[12] For Wilderson, any apparent political gains made by the black performance nevertheless leave the substructures of antiblackness intact; in short, Hartman's "space for action" is always already compromised—there simply is no free space for blackness in a world governed by whiteness. After all, Jay-Z's refrain "Can I live?" remains a question, and there is no shortage of evidence suggesting that blackness is very much still on the run; as such, hip hop may be understood not only as a performance of black (social) life but also, like afropessimism itself, as a valuable critical commentary on its relative possibility or impossibility.

Wilderson puts it bluntly at the end of "Grammar and Ghosts": "This is the problem that performance studies has yet to work through: "*How*, or more to the point, *why* does one perform in and for a world that has forced upon one cartographic and temporal injunctions that are always already operative at every scale, from the body to the village to the nation to the continent to the diaspora? Who is served by [...] this easy

---

[9] Saidiya Hartman, *Scenes of Subjection* (Oxford: Oxford University Press, 1997), 8.

[10] Hartman, *Scenes of Subjection*, 8.

[11] See, for instance, Michael Eric Dyson, "The Culture of Hip-Hop," in *That's the Joint: The Hip-Hop Studies Reader*, eds. Murray Forman and Mark Anthony Neal (New York: Routledge, 2004), 61.

[12] Wilderson, "Grammar and Ghosts," 121.

grammatical join of art and liberation?"[13] Every black performance, Wilderson says, is "haunted by the grammar and ghosts of Africa's structural violence," and this haunting prevents the black performance from achieving the one thing structural change of the kind imagined by Wilderson requires, namely, what he calls "direct reflection."[14]

Where Wilderson describes the problem as it animates or, rather, fails to animate the field of performance studies, P. Khalil Saucier and Tryon Woods explore the same missed opportunity as it is made manifest in critical studies of hip hop: "Hip hop studies will remain utterly wretched unless it comes to terms with the structure of gratuitous violence in which it exists. In order to chart an ethical future, hip hop studies must *become* black studies, and in so doing, confront the ways in which black existence in an anti-black world—in other words, a universe where black life is structurally impermissible—is bound up with [...] a fugitive life 'lived in loss.'"[15] According to Saucier and Woods, hip hop studies too routinely embraces the performance of black pathology at the expense of taking head on the structural conditions that lead to the pathology in the first place; consequently, they challenge hip hop studies, in becoming *black* studies, to come to terms with the *structure*, instead of the *performance*, of black life.[16]

To be sure, however, whether we trace hip hop's origins to a movement or a moment, hip hop already accomplishes such a *coming to terms* in itself.[17] On the one hand, hip hop is understood to have begun with the spontaneous creative decisions of DJ's like Kool Herc and Kool DJ Dee to "talk" over dance records at disco after-parties in early 1970's New York City. The most visible and influential of these early innovators, Afrika Bambaataa, imagined hip hop as a means of inspiring hope in the urban black community and famously expressed the goals of the new cultural movement as "peace, love, unity, and having fun,"[18] goals that are playfully reinforced throughout the early years of the genre and, most notably, at the end of the decade with the appearance of The Sugar Hill Gang's

[13] Wilderson, "Grammar and Ghosts," 124. Emphasis added.

[14] Wilderson, "Grammar and Ghosts," 121, 122–3.

[15] P. Khalil Saucier and Tryon P. Woods, "Hip Hop Studies in Black," *Journal of Popular Music Studies* 26, no. 2–3 (2014): 285.

[16] Saucier and Woods, "Hip Hop Studies," 274.

[17] Michael Eric Dyson also contrasts these two beginnings. See Dyson, "Hip-Hop," 61–2.

[18] Qtd. in Greg Thomas, *Hip Hop Revolution in the Flesh: Power, Knowledge, and Pleasure in Lil' Kim's Lyricism* (New York: Palgrave Macmillan, 2009), 1.

"Rapper's Delight," hip hop's first broad commercial success and the fist hip hop song to appear on the Billboard Top 100: "My name is Wonder Mike/and I'd like to say Hello/to the white, to the black/the red and the brown/the purple and yellow." In keeping with Hartman's simultaneity, the playfulness so typical of these early years may be viewed as reinforcing the claims of antiblackness and/or embraced as fundamental to black resistance.

Insofar as this joy may be likened to the historical coping associated with black spirituals and the blues, and one would be justified in including the abstractions and popular concessions of jazz and R&B as well, the rapper's delight not only remains tethered to those relations of domination to which it owes its existence, but those relations appear structurally designed to tolerate it. At the same time, such joy has always been indispensable for black survival, an affirmation of black experience amidst the negations of antiblackness, carrying within it the promise of a free black cultural, social, and political life.[19] After all, Bambaataa and the early innovators clearly conceived of hip hop as a protest of existing conditions and knew the public joy it inspired was irrevocably linked to the social, economic, and technological scarcity out of which it emerged and that the power of black joy lay as much in its implausibility as in its irrepressibility.[20] As critical as it is to black survival, however, Wilderson warns readers that the performance of black joy poses no immediate threat to the structural persistence of antiblackness, but instead only reinforces black social death and the Heideggerian premise, on which Moten's case relies, that the possibility of a black *Dasein* [*being-there*] remains haunted by its own impossibility.[21]

On the other hand, and to some extent as a result of the optimism associated with the early days of the genre, this historical scale begins to tip with the advent of hip hop. In another story of hip hop's origins, critics and historians cite the 1982 release of Grandmaster Flash and the Furious Five's "The Message,"[22] which, more so than any effort before it, announces in its notorious first line—"Broken glass, everywhere!"—the miserable conditions of modern black urban life and makes the material

[19] See, for example, James H. Cone, *The Spirituals and the Blues* (New York: Orbis, 1972).
[20] See, for example, Greg Dimitriadis, "Hip-Hop: From Live Performance to Mediated Narrative," in *That's the Joint: The Hip-Hop Studies Reader*, eds. Murray Forman and Mark Anthony Neal (New York: Routledge, 2004), 421–2.
[21] Martin Heidegger, *Being and Time*, trans. John Macquarrie and Edward Robinson (Oxford: Blackwell, 1962), 294; see also Moten, "Case," 182–87.
[22] See, for example, Dyson, "Hip-hop," 61–2.

and psychological despair of the black community a part of the public record for the first time in the genre's history. Beyond this critical acknowledgment, however, "The Message" strikes an entirely new tone with its indelible refrain—"Don't push me/cuz I'm close to the edge." The message in "The Message" inaugurates an entirely new basis for hip hop's joy, namely, the joy of its powerful and independent repositioning over and against whiteness, an early warning shot by that genre that one may argue outmaneuvers the strict limits of the slave performance.

Whichever origin myth one prefers, from its very beginning hip hop faces head on the structural barriers that define black existence, and hip hop continues far past its origins to draw attention to and contest these structural inequities, effectively mapping the edge of a claustrophobic boundary that separates black social life from white civil society. While critics, such as Mark Anthony Neal and Michael Eric Dyson, are right that hip hop is not the first black musical genre to speak truth to power,[23] it is the only musical genre that may be described, in itself, as a manner of speaking this truth. As such, a direct line may be drawn from "The Message" to the following examples (and so many others like it), and, along the way, hip hop becomes indistinguishable from the complaint itself:

Too $hort, "The Ghetto," Short Dog's in the House (1990)	Notorious BIG, "Suicidal Thoughts," Ready to Die (1994)	Nas, "Last Words," Nastradamus (1999)
Even though the streets are bumpy lights burned out dope fiends die with a pipe in their mouth old school buddies not doing it right every day's the same and it's the same every night	When I die, fuck it I wanna go to hell cuz I'm a piece of shit it ain't hard to fucking tell It don't make sense going to heaven with the goody-goodies dressed in white I like black Timbs and black hoodies	I'm a prison cell six-by-nine livin' hell stone wall, metal bars for the gods in jail My nickname's the can the slammer, big house I'm the place many fear cuz there's no way out

In all of these examples, hip hop bluntly acknowledges the structural violence that defines urban black life, and consequently highlights precisely what Wilderson says is really wanted of black art and what Saucier and Woods claim is wanted in hip hop studies, that is, a more "direct

---

[23] Dyson, "Hip-Hop," 64–5. See also Michael Anthony Neal, *What the Music Said: Black Popular Music and Black Public Culture* (New York: Routledge, 1999).

reflection" on hip hop's relationship to and engagement with the structural basis and limitations of black (social) life. There is, after all, no "easy grammatical join of art and liberation" at work in "The Message," and, as circumstances escalate with the maturation of the form, one would be hard-pressed to find more effective examples of such "direct reflection," in which the lines between art and life are so fundamentally crossed, than in Too $hort's "streets," Biggie's self-loathing, or Nas' "prison cell."

Even if one admits those attributes of hip hop that set it apart from other black musical traditions, Wilderson's suspicions surrounding the degree to which such performativity positively alters the "relations of domination" in which it is caught up remain justified. Nevertheless, Hartmann's "space for action"; Jared Sexton's forceful reminder that black life, as impermissible as it may be, is nevertheless *lived*[24]; and Wilderson's belief that performance and ontology do, in fact, meet, amount to a shared, albeit very cautious, optimism that implies a transformative black aesthetic and the possibility, not the impossibility (as one might expect), of black life. According to afropessimism, what is wanted is a more direct critical engagement with the implications *for* black life of the antagonism itself—what Frank Wilderson refers to, in contrast to the "liberation" model, as a model of "understanding" and what Sexton refers to as the necessity of "getting inside [blackness]."[25] It is, then, within the context of Moten's positive assessment of the "fugitive" performance and Wilderson's stinging critique of black performativity that Sexton asks whether a black art that "affirms (social) life can avoid the thanatological dead end if it does not will its own (social) death"[26] and suggests that such a will, situated as it is at the edge of its own existence, is forced to take an unprecedented *turn* toward itself: "In a world structured by the twin axioms of white superiority and black inferiority, of white existence and black nonexistence [...] the zero degree of transformation is the turn toward blackness."[27] Thus just as "The Message" may be considered a historical turning point for the genre, it also exemplifies a kind of turning in itself that echoes not only across the genre but also in Sexton's "zero degree of transformation" that coincides with "the turn toward blackness."

[24] Sexton, "Social Life," 28–9.
[25] Sexton, "Social Life," 24.
[26] Sexton, "Social Life," 28–29.
[27] Sexton, "Social Life," 27.

Simply put, what is wanted by afropessimism is the achievement of the understanding that the way *out* for blackness is *in*. And this curious resolution invites an answer to Sexton's challenge to his readers to conceive of black life as taking place in "a world in which the world does not live" and to accept afropessimism as "'not but nothing other than' black optimism": "Black life is not lived in the world that the world lives in [...]. That's the whole point of the enterprise at some level. It is all about the implications of this agreed-upon point where arguments (should) begin, but they cannot (yet) proceed."[28] In turn, it also invites an answer to Wilderson's question of how an authentic black performance is possible, much less wanted, "*in* and *for* a world that has forced upon one cartographic and temporal injunctions that are always already operative at every scale."[29] The answer, it seems, is that it isn't, but this doesn't render black life also impossible since Sexton conceives for us a black life and art that takes place neither *in* nor *for* a non- or antiblack world, but rather *in* and *for* a world in which that world does not live, a black world, and it is, consequently and following both Sexton's and hip hop's clearing, only in or out of *this* world that an authentic black freedom and optimism can position itself to emerge.

THE TURN TOWARD BLACKNESS

In Sexton's turn, hip hop performativity can be said to "come to terms with the structure of gratuitous violence,"[30] to become black studies, and to give voice to the "emergence and being"[31] of a political ontology that is no longer an ontology of the slave. Insofar as acts of resistance are always performative and, following Hartman, "acquire their character from [...] relations [of domination], and vice-versa,"[32] these acts are nevertheless not prevented from shaping an independent subjective and social relation to the dominant reality and, in effect, acquiring a freedom and movement, even a *world*, perhaps, that in another world is denied to them. In fact, hip hop would appear to obtain its cultural and political force from its being jammed up at this confluence or "gathering"[33] where Wilderson says

28 Sexton, "Social Life," 28–9.
29 Wilderson, "Grammar and Ghosts," 124.
30 Saucier and Woods, "Hip Hop Studies," 285.
31 Wilderson, "Grammar and Ghosts," 119.
32 Hartman, *Scenes*, 8.
33 Wilderson, "Grammar and Ghosts," 122. Also qtd. in Sexton, "Social Life," 1.

performance and ontology intersect and where Sexton suspects blackness is coerced into a turn toward itself.

This turning is especially visible at the center of tracks like The Coup's "Not yet Free" (1993). After having spelled out the day-to-day struggle of black life ("In this land/I can't stand or sit/and not get shit thrown up in my face"), Boots Riley protests:

> *Ni****, thugs, dope dealers, and pimps,*
> *basketball players, rap stars and simps:*
> That's what little black boys are made of.
>
> *Sluts, hos, and press the naps around your neck,*
> *broads pop that coochie, bitches, stay in check:*
> That's what little black girls are made of.
>
> But if we're made of that
> who made us
> and what can we do to change us?

Certainly a stereotypical blackness is registered in this performance, one that is tragically internalized by the black community but scripted outside of it under the authority and direction of a violent and oppressive system of antiblackness ("I got a mirror in my pocket/and I practice looking hard"). At the same time, the recognition of the script handed down to blackness by whiteness and of another collective self-struggling to navigate the imposition does more than reinforce a black double-consciousness; rather, it achieves a formidable counter-stance.[34] The Coup, and hip hop more broadly, exposes the imposition *as* script, enlisting its listeners and, by extension, the black community to rewrite the script anew and confront the structural antagonism itself in such a way called for by afropessimism insofar as in this verse what it means to *do* blackness and what it means to *be* black do, in fact, and rather self-consciously, *meet.*

Moreover, it is in this promise of the meeting, at the historical crossing paths of blackness with itself, that both Wilderson and artists like The Coup evince an optimism not unlike Sexton's faith in the turn toward blackness. Consequently, the question of how one might imagine the possibility of black social life is the right question to ask—against the backdrop of afropessimism's alleged claim that "there is no black (social)

---

[34] Greg Thomas' *Hip-Hop Revolution in the Flesh* says as much in his narrower study of Lil' Kim's lyricism.

life,"[35] Moten asks his readers in "The Case of Blackness" to "fathom a [black] social life that tends toward death, that enacts a kind of being-toward-death, and which, because of such tendency and enactment, maintains a terribly beautiful vitality?"[36] As afropessimism insists, however, this question cannot be asked at the expense of the afropessimist denial but must always be envisioned against the lived reality that "black life does not live in the world that the world lives in."[37] In other words, only once the end (or social death) of blackness has been announced (This is an "agreed upon point," after all)[38] can the social life of blackness be articulated for the first time. And so we find ourselves with the afropessimists, and, not coincidentally, with hip hop, as much at the beginning of blackness as at the end of it.

We also find ourselves still grappling with the question of how such an emergence is to be imagined against its own structural impossibility, or how a fugitive life, in turning toward itself, might become something other than it already is. Deleuze and Guattari's observation in *A Thousand Plateaus* that "European racism as the white man's claim has never operated by exclusion, or by the designation of someone as Other"[39] sheds light on these questions, especially as they reinforce Wilderson's and Sexton's guarded optimism. Following Deleuze and Guattari, the impossibility of black life lies not so much in its exclusion from but in its inclusion in "a world structured by the twin axioms of white superiority and black inferiority."[40] According to afropessimism, the inseparability of these "twin axioms" is the legacy of slavery and the basis of the structural impossibility of black social life. As a result, and as The Coup's "Not Yet Free" demonstrates, Sexton's turn toward blackness can be more precisely grasped as a turning away not from the antagonism as such but away from the pathology generated in it, becoming something *other* than "black" for the first time insofar as this, Deleuze and Guattari argue, is the name of the "impurity conferred upon it by a system of domination."[41]

[35] Sexton, "Social Life," 28.
[36] Moten, "Case," 188.
[37] Sexton, "Social Life," 28.
[38] Sexton, "Social Life," 29.
[39] Gilles Deleuze and Felix Guattari, *A Thousand Plateaus* (Minneapolis: Minnesota UP, 1987), 178.
[40] Sexton, "Social Life," 27.
[41] Deleuze and Guattari, *Plateaus*, 379.

It is in *this* otherness, then, that an authentic black freedom comes to the surface, moves on its own, and not according to but still always against and alongside the dictates of white power, privilege, and authority. Sexton, whose work is close kin to Wilderson's, suggests it is precisely here, on the point of what afropessimism makes possible, that arguments should begin, that an authentic black optimism can be felt.[42] Further, such a beginning must necessarily move beyond Marxist or post-colonial *ressentiment* toward what Wilderson calls *critique*, where the long process of abolition can be completed, an enduring process that is no longer caught up in the affairs of the master, but, rather, as Deleuze and Guattari suggest, involves a "self-destruction" that has "nothing to do with the death drive."[43] Within the scope of Deleuze and Guattari's critical race theory, the black world described by Sexton, in which the world does not live, is not the "thanatological dead end"[44] of social death that he warns about, but rather the world of black social life opened up after the impasse has been reached, which is also to say, in blackness's willing the death of one history through what Wilderson refers to as the "grammar"[45] of another's emergence. In this way Sexton's transformative aesthetic that has blackness turning toward itself invites us to view hip hop as the optimistic—grammatical, if you will—movement of blackness nearer to itself.

Achieving this proximity to blackness begins with achieving a radical proximity to the structural negation that makes blackness what it *appears* to be. Such an engagement, though, requires not only that a fugitive blackness stops fleeing, but also that it turns around—both toward the source of that negation and toward itself in the negation. As demonstrated above, hip hop closes this distance from its earliest days, but then it must also reject what it finds there and turn upon the negation in such a way that blurs the line between black performance and black lived experience and returns body and voice to an autonomous blackness asserting its *being* against the reality of its erasure:

---

[42] Sexton, "Social Life," 29.
[43] Deleuze and Guattari, *Plateaus*, 160.
[44] Sexton, "Social Life," 16.
[45] Wilderson, "Grammar and Ghosts," 119.

Public Enemy, "Don't Believe the Hype," It Takes Nation of Millions to Hold Us Back (1988)	NWA, "Fuck the Police," Straight outta Compton (1988)	Wu-Tang Clan, ODB, "Reunited," Wu-Tang Forever I (1997)
Number one, not born to run, about the gun, I wasn't licensed to have one The minute they see me, fear me, I'm the epitome of 'public enemy'	Fuck that shit cuz I ain't the one for a punk motherfucker with a badge and a gun to be beatin' on I'm a sniper with a hell of a scope Taking out a cop or two they can't cope with me […] So I'ma turn it around Put in my clip, yo, and this is the sound	My name's Black You worms wanna play in my dirt? Bitch stop!

Another direct line may be drawn from "The Message" to these examples in which what is mostly reinforced is the emergent nature and character of hip hop's multivalent turn(s) toward blackness and the way in which blackness in hip hop, in the turn toward itself, becomes something else altogether.

On the one hand, in "Don't Believe the Hype" Public Enemy (PE) is "back" again, a "sequel"—in this world, what it means to be black, what little black boys and girls are made of, is tied to the historical mechanics of antiblackness: "They see me/fear me/I'm the epitome/of 'public enemy.'" On the other hand, the track's opening lines quite literally catch listeners "lookin' for the same thing," when, as Public Enemy points out, "It's a new thing." Here hip hop, and, by extension, the blackness expressed in it, is no longer "born to run." It is not so much late in history as right on time, a brand new thing, and, as such, invokes something *other* than performance since to perform blackness means, in part, to reiterate an inherited identity or value that has been maintained and developed over time and, perhaps most importantly, that has been bestowed upon the performer from the outside.[46] After all, it is precisely this *hype* about what it means to be black—"see me/fear me"—in which Public Enemy implores its listeners *not* to believe. If "Don't Believe the Hype" turns toward blackness in its turn against the white script, elsewhere on this legendary LP, "Louder than a Bomb" turns toward blackness in an even more direct sense. While the song also stakes out its claim at the end of a long tradition, both old and new ("The style is wild/but don't treat me like a

---

[46] Judith Butler, *Gender Trouble: Feminism and the Subversion of Identity* (New York: Routledge, 2002), 33.

stepchild"), blackness is "on file" in this example not because it is a public enemy, but rather because "Our status is the saddest/And I care where you at, Black."

One sees these deliberate strategies at work, too, in NWA's violent repositioning over and against the police. When Ice Cube asserts his dignity and independence ("I ain't the one [...]/to be beating on") or when, on the same track, Easy E declares, "My identity itself causes violence," hip hop finds itself at that busy crossing where white and black scripts overlap and black performance and identity converge. Just as Public Enemy is no longer "born to run," and whereas all earlier black musical traditions are assessed as ways of coping with antiblackness, MC Ren announces the incapacity of white power to "cope" with the appearance of this new iteration of blackness ("They can't cope with me"). Simultaneously, MC Ren quite literally stops running and turns around ("So I'ma *turn it around*/Put in my clip, yo/and *this is the sound*") in a move that arguably aligns this turning with a brand new positioning of black subjectivity over and against antiblackness and with the metaphorical sound of the gun blast, that is to say, with hip hop music and culture and the birth of "gangsta" rap.

On the surface, Old Dirty Bastard's (ODB) verse clearly reflects the "gratuitous violence in which [hip hop] exists,"[47] and he plays the role of the quintessential antagonist in the plot of white reality well enough, but it is not this tethering that stands out in his performance. Indeed, we are quite far removed from the buoyant, good-humored introductions of "Rappers Delight"—"My name is known/all of the world/by all the foxy ladies/and the pretty girls," and ODB's tragic premise assumes he is already dead, a social corpse he calls by its/his name ("My name's Black"). Still, ODB's introduction is as much a potent counter-performance, one he emphasizes as the verse continues ("Unglove the noose/Watch a nigga transfuse"), as it is a *mere* performance of an antiblack pathology. The otherwise very literal dead end signaled in the sharp finality and recognition of the premise, "My name's Black," opens at the same time toward an enigmatic subjectivity and exaggerated indecipherability for which ODB is well-known and that in its (only apparently) parodic enactment of blackness manifests as a constant threat to white capacity through which both abolition and a particular kind of black social life is realized. Always

---

[47] Saucier and Woods, "Hip Hop Studies," 285.

breaking through the surface of ODB's performance is the voice and fig-ure of a black protagonist that owes nothing to the white script and involves an emphatic self-overcoming of "blackness" that begins not with evasion but with a willing encounter with what it means to *be* toward death. In this way hip hop performativity actively resists speaking in or for an antiblack world—"You worms wanna play in my dirt? Bitch stop!"[48]

So it is that hip hop performativity coincides with Sexton's "turn toward blackness" and as such is tantamount to a *counter*-performance, a turning inward toward a novel and more immediate confrontation with itself and a turning around toward a fresh black agency that in yet another way frac-tures the simultaneity of the slave performance. Certainly one could argue this re-scripting or reterritorialization of blackness undoes the perfor-mance in a much more absolute sense. Despite the violence, both real and imagined, that accompanies the turn, hip hop enters the history of dis-course surrounding the nature and character of black life with an optimis-tic vitality that permeates every production. After all, ODB's unique style famously "has no father" ("Interlude," *36 Chambers*) and thus operates independently of the father's authority; hip hop, in a similar denial, func-tions independently of the authority of both black and white performance traditions even as it (mis)appropriates them and in doing so bastardizes what Moten calls the "natal occasion" of blackness, black captivity, and black artistic traditions. In fact, even when hip hop was still just a point of light in the eye of the culture, and in what is nevertheless one of the most emphatic expressions of this overcoming or turning toward, The Last Poets demand something like a social life out of social death, a blackness *after* blackness: "Die nigga, so black folks can take over" (but not *real* n*****, since, as the eponymous track by NWA insists, "real ni**** never die").

In the end, ODB's exaggerated persona is indicative of possibility, not impossibility, and one finds a similar optimism in the last words of Nas' dying slave, "I'ma keep sayin' ..." and in Chuck D's reminder at the beginning of "Don't Believe the Hype," "*YES!/*was the start of my last jam." In these examples and across the lyrical landscape of classical hip-hop one witnesses a new blackness speaking *of* itself *for* itself and "out of

---

[48] That hip hop performativity is so closely linked to black ontologies certainly complicates things, but this difficulty is a vital symptom of their inseparability and a core function of the genre.

the possibilities embedded in a social *life*" that is hip hop music and culture.[49] Such a circumstance places us alongside the preoccupations of the afropessimists, for whom becoming something other than *black*, insofar as this is the name of the "impurity conferred upon it by a system of domination,"[50] is the only thing that breaks the antagonism apart; accordingly, the way to move past the afterlife of slavery is to destabilize the historically fortified structures of antiblackness and enter the afterlife of *blackness* itself, since, as the examples above demonstrate, blackness can always find itself situated at the edge of an entirely new significance and signification.

COUNTER-PERFORMANCE AS PRAXIS

Sylvia Wynter's original thesis redefines blackness, and what it means to be human, as *praxis* and sheds even more light on the nature of hip hop's counter-performative turn toward blackness.[51] The way in which Wynter's thought has been deployed to locate black life in black music is altogether kindred with Moten's objectives in *In the Break* and "The Case of Blackness" and resonates directly with Sexton's question of whether an aesthetic that "affirms (social) life can avoid the thanatological dead end if it does not will its own (social) death."[52] For Wynter, "[B]lack cultural production writes scientific and disciplinary knowledge anew, as necessarily a human project,"[53] and Wynter's brand of "[b]lack humanism disenchants 'Man as Man,' bringing 'into being different modes of the *human*' because it deploys the very formulation of 'man' as catachresis."[54]

Wynter and others, like Kodwo Eshun, view black music as a potential staging ground for a black humanity that is otherwise obstructed from *being* by antiblackness. As Katherine McKittrick and Alexander Weheliye point out, this obstruction does not necessarily imply black nonexistence but rather a black *Dasein* or *being-there*, for whom its being [black] is an

---

[49] Moten, "Case," 192.

[50] Deleuze and Guattari, *Plateaus*, 160.

[51] See Katherine McKittrick and Sylvia Wynter, *Sylvia Wynter: On Being Human as Praxis*, ed. Katherine McKittrick, New York, USA: Duke University Press, 2015.

[52] Sexton, "Social Life," 28–9.

[53] Katherine McKittrick and Sylvia Wynter, *Sylvia Wynter: On Being Human as Praxis*, ed. Katherine McKittrick, (New York: Duke University Press, 2015), 142–63. See also Sexton, "Social Life," 28.

[54] Weheliye, "Feenin'," 27.

issue.[55] As her phenomenological approach would have it, Wynter maintains that such a being is always being-in-the-world and thus requires a special proximity insofar as blackness is the product of both an individual and collective "self-making."[56] Mos Def's 2004 remix of Grandmaster Flash and the Furious Five's chorus from "The Message" is an extraordinary example of a critical evolution in the turn toward blackness and of the proximity achieved in it, where the darkened edge of a world that pushes blackness to the margins gives way to a world that revolves absolutely around it: "Don't push me/cuz I'm close to the …/streets, to the beats/ the bitches, the niggas/the women, the children/the workers, the addicts/ the killers, the dealers […]/and that's close."

Not only is such proximity called for in Sexton's turn *toward* blackness, but what else is hip hop if not the product of a self-making that takes place in blackness's turn toward itself, or what Deleuze and Guattari might call a black lodging in/on the "white face" that gathers its strength and virtue by "tearing the conscious away from the subject in order to make it a means of exploration, tearing the unconscious away from signifiance (*sic*) and interpretation in order to make it a veritable production"[57] and/or praxis? In fact, nothing quite conflates *being* and *doing* blackness like the "veritable production[s]" of black voices that hip hop, essentially, *is*, and to which every lyrical flow always refers. Every written/recorded rap, after all, invokes a memory of itself *as free*style, and nothing links the performance of blackness in hip hop more clearly and directly with the structural "noose of slavery" and the ontological status of the black subject than the notation at the end of The Coup's "Not Yet Free": "No, this is not yet freestyle/cuz we are not yet free." From Wynter's perspective the distinction between what it means to *be* black and what it means to *do* blackness falls away and collapses in the category of praxis, through which an authentic black humanity is quite literally *made* intelligible in and for itself.

Both the turn toward blackness and the counter-performative in the turn can be seen operating across hip hop, where what is reinforced is the instigation of a black subjectivity through which a specifically black "grammar of emergence and being" is articulated. On Method Man and Redman's appropriately titled *Blackout!* (1999), Streetlife raps:

---

[55] Heidegger famously says of Dasein that it may be "distinguished by the fact that, in its very Being, that Being is an *issue* for it." (BoT 32)

[56] Thomas, *Revolution*, 13–14.

[57] Deleuze and Guattari, *Plateaus*, 160.

I'm the cynical, lyrical, rap individual
On my death bed I spit sick flows that's critical
I'm not a fan of this
I'm a mic vandalist, thug therapist
My clan's too original [...]
Who wanna come test, lick the sweat from my genitals
We can get off the mic and get a little physical

In this verse, as in so many others, the mic and the hip hop performance with which it is associated translates social death into social life, literally and figuratively amplifying black existence. As with MC culture, generally speaking, here again Streetlife inevitably acknowledges the past-less nature of his flow ("My clan's too original"), further exemplifying the way in which a rap aesthetic inaugurates a specific and original way of being in the world *as* catachresis. The names of this new black subject proliferate throughout the greater sequence—*mic vandalist, thug therapist, rhyme writer, hip hop provider, live wire*, etc. Further, just as ODB's double-edged premise ("My name's Black/You worms wanna play in my dirt?") and Nas' last words (I'ma keep sayin'") *begin* at the end—here a "cynical, lyrical, rap individual" is *born* on his "deathbed spit[tin'] sick flows that's critical."

The routine analogy in hip hop culture that links the mic with black lived experience stages the drama of an original black experience and pleasure that is first and foremost *voiced* and *heard*. Such an emphasis can also be seen in Method Man's verse on the same track, "It ain't your grand-daddy's music/It's hip hop/Coming through your woofer like a mule-kick/100,000 watts", or, perhaps most famously, in DJ Kool's 1996 rap anthem "Let me clear my throat ...." Through this performative amplification blackness is transformed into an assertive and positive ontology, confirming Lewis Gordon's insistence that the best way to resist antiblackness is to *be black*, which is just another kind of turning toward.[58] After all, Method Man reminds us elsewhere on *Blackout!* that he will always "live ghetto, stay ghetto, pants sagging, teeth yellow," that he's "blacker than the blackest stallion," or, maybe, "like ODB, too black."

---

[58] Lewis Gordon, "Black Existence in Philosophy and Culture," *Diogenes*, 59.3–4 (2014): 96–105.

Alongside hip hop's amplification of the black voice, Streetlife's rap commentary also betrays the understanding on the part of many rappers that what they are up to is precisely *not* performance. Streetlife not only unequivocally rejects the label ("I'm not a fan of this"), but he also reminds the listener that the space between the hip hop performance and black lived experience is one that is easily crossed ("We can get off the mic and get a little physical"). Everywhere in hip hop, rap's probing inquiry into the status of black social life is enlisted to move past the limits of performance toward a black lived experience, and this observation effectively responds to Wilderson's critique of black performance and should go some way toward revitalizing the authenticity debates about the implications of hip hop's constant reminder to "keep it real":

Mobb Deep, "Shook Ones," Infamous (1995)	Jay Z, "Where I'm From," In My Lifetime, Vol. 1 (1997)	Jaylib, "Survival Test," Champion Sound (2003)
For every rhyme I write it's 25 to life Yo, it's a must in gats we trust safeguardin' my life Ain't no time for hesitation That only leads to incarceration You don't know me There's no relation	Your word was everything so everything you said you'd do you did it Couldn't talk about it if you ain't lived it I'm from where niggas pull your card and argue all day about who's the best MC Biggie, Jay-Z, or Nas?	You don't wanna be without here Niggas ain't giving a fuck they'll pull it out here [...] How a lotta blood get spilled out here It's fucked up, but it's real out here Is that how it is out there? Shit don't make sense out here

In "Where I'm From" Jay-Z offers a riveting sketch of black life in the NYC neighborhood where he grew up. In addition to painting a picture of a "world in which the world does not live" ("I'm from where the other guys don't walk too much), "Where I'm from" blurs the line between the hip hop performance and black lived experience in at least two ways. Jay-Z is able to "talk about it" precisely because he has "lived it," and he notes the inseparability of the other world in which he lives and the *talking* about it, which is to say, of course, hip hop itself—"I'm from where niggas pull your card/And argue all day about who's the best MC/Biggie, Jay-Z or Nas?" Similarly, J Dilla admits "[i]t's fucked up, but it's real out here," and Mobb Deep's seminal "Shook Ones" begins with the listener "stuck off the realness" and a dedication of their "performance" not to fans but to "real niggas who ain't got no feelings." In Mobb Deep's anthem, especially, the boundary between art and life is thoroughly erased. Prodigy warns his audience, "Now take these words home and think it through, or the next rhyme I write might be about you," while Havoc insists, "For every rhyme I write it's 25 to life." In all these examples performance itself would appear every bit as "shook" as those real life "shook ones" the Mobb Deep track memorializes. In each case rap transcends the limits of performance toward a taking over of what it means, as Moten suggests, to *be* toward death, all of which amounts to a counter-performance and counter-discourse that in the turn toward blackness, in the head on engagement with its own social death, finds itself somewhere in the difference between what J Dilla calls "here" and "there."

This active acknowledgment (that is at the same time a production) of the difference between the world of whiteness and the world "where the others guys don't walk too much" indeed reinforces the idea of blackness as "catachresis,"[59] conveying a specific and felt black self-consciousness and pleasure exposed when hip hop *becomes* black. As such, it also goes some way toward explaining how hip hop, as counter-performance, undertakes the difficult task of acquiring what Wilderson cites as being essential to black ontological and political autonomy, namely, "differentiation or self-knowledge,"[60] and how hip hop makes plain what Wynter describes as *another* humanity writing "scientific and disciplinary knowledge anew."

In addition to the collapse of the barrier between stage and reality, a collapsing that ties the black performance directly to the possibility of black freedom, hip hop's emphasis on the blackness of this freedom points to something untranslatable in what is given, an alterity inaccessible to the non-black spectator that supports a uniquely black subjectivity and lived experience forcefully positioned against a dominant language and reality. "Shit don't make sense out here," J Dilla says; between "here" and "there," Mobb Deep asserts, "You don't know me/There's no relation," and even much newer artists, such as Kendrick Lamar, continue to register this differentiation and the esoteric knowledge that accompanies it: "This feeling is unmatched, brought to you by adrenaline and good rap [...] We don't share the same synonym, fall back."

To be sure, the Wu-Tang Clan appears especially committed to such a (re)cognition:

---

[59] Weheliye, "Feenin'," 27.
[60] Wilderson, "Grammar and Ghosts," 122.

Wu-Tang Clan, "Triumph," Wu-Tang Forever II (1997)	Wu-Tang Clan, "Reunited," Wu-Tang Forever II (1997)
Inspectah Deck I bomb atomically Socrates' philosophies and hypotheses can't define how I be droppin' these mockeries Lyrically perform armed robberies Possibly they spotted me	Uncompleted missions, throw in your best known compositions You couldn't add it up if you mastered addition How can I put it? Life is like video footage hard to edit Directors, they never understood it

Earlier ODB recovered in his world what, in another world, had been rejected (My name's Black!) and simultaneously evicted potential interlopers ("You worms wanna play in my dirt? Bitch stop!"). The hyper unintelligibility that is the mark of his "fatherless' style puts blackness out of the reach of both whiteness and the structural antagonism constructed around it, again showing that blackness, like the flow, is indeed "hard to capture." On the surface, Inspectah Deck's remarkable opening salvo in "Triumph" would appear to bring us full circle insofar as it may be said to reinforce the fugitive trope that has the black subject always *on the run* ("Lyrically perform armed robberies/possibly they spotted me"). However, a closer look reveals a novel epistemology that not only belongs wholly to blackness in and for itself but that stands out for its emphasis on white incapacity ("Socrates philosophies [...] can't define how I be droppin' these mockeries"). Meanwhile, GZA ("You couldn't add it up/if you mastered addition") and RZA ("Directors, they never understood it") only reinforce this incapacity and in the process further undermine the structural integrity of the antagonism built around the "twin axioms of white existence and black nonexistence." And, finally, elsewhere on the same LP, ODB finds yet another way to draw the listener's attention to this vital "differentiation" that ultimately frees blackness from the grip of white power: "Just like Black shoe fit/If you can't wear it/Well, don't fuck with it." The implication is that blackness evades white capture here not because blackness is *on the run* from but rather because it lies fundamentally *beyond the grasp* of whiteness.

The productive tension here between an ontology of black art/life, its right to exist, and the administrative, historical (white) world in which it appears, that prohibits its existence, and thus against which black life/art always measures its powers *to be*, mirrors Moten's critical distinction between Fanon's infamous conception of blackness as "an object in the midst of other objects"[61] and a black *Dasein* or social-ontological agency that exceeds this objectivity, a difference between the made thing, blackness as it is rendered by whiteness, and the thing/world of its making, or the turning toward blackness in and for itself.[62] It also clarifies, here at the end, the difference between blackness as the made thing in a world *from* which blackness, according to Wilderson, has been removed and in which it is under constant and categorical assault, and Sexton's world "in which the world does not live," the world not *from* which blackness has been removed but *toward* which it has removed itself in its "self-making," a world of its own.

Hip hop, it can be said, transforms black subjected-ness into the "aesthetic sociality"[63] of a world that not only *belongs* to blackness and black social life, but that gave/gives life to this modern black world "in which the world does not live." In doing so, hip hop also transforms what it means to be black from an affirmation of white capacity into a radical affirmation of black life, or, Sexton suggests, "a radical negation of antiblackness."[64] The result is both a musical genre indistinguishable from the lived reality it performs and an irrevocable and comprehensive revelation of black personal and social knowledge, as Notorious BIG explains it so memorably at the end of "Juicy" on his 1994 debut album, *Ready to Die*: "If you don't know, now you know, nigga."

Much more recently, but no less strikingly, Kendrick Lamar says the same thing on *To Pimp a Butterfly* (2015):

> I know everything, I know everything
> Know myself
> I know morality, spirituality, good and bad health
> I know fatality might haunt you
> I know everything, I know Compton
> I know street shit, I know shit that's conscious, I know everything [...]
> I know everything, I know history
> I know the universe works mentally [...]
>
> I know how people work, I know the price of life
> I'm knowin' how much it's worth

---

[61] Qtd. in Jared Sexton and Huey Copeland, "Raw Life: An Introduction," *Qui Parle* (2003): 53.
[62] Moten, "Case," 182.
[63] Moten, "Case," 192.
[64] Sexton, "Social Life."

I know what I know and I know it well
Not to ever forget until I realized I didn't know shit
The day I came home.

Through the counter-performance, or a hip hop praxis, a black *Dasein* is revealed, and in the turn toward itself blackness comes *to know* itself through the structural violence at the ground of its existence. Kendrick Lamar's coming home is a (re)turn toward the long-obscured black (social) self *as* being-toward-death, and, alongside hip hop itself, suggests a collective *being toward* that is open-ended and consequently critically different from the "thanatological dead end" of Heideggerian finitude. And this is how afropessimism conveys a dynamic optimism in the turn toward blackness that in its "radical affirmation of a blackened world" is both a turning *other* for the first time *and* a turn (again) toward its own humanity and self-actualization.

CONCLUSION

As much as these conclusions and the bulk of the critical theory surrounding the possibility or impossibility of black existence reflect a distinctly Heideggerian legacy, we may do well to end with a brief reference to the Frankfurt School, in particular Theodor Adorno's take on the end of art and philosophy (incidentally, but for different reasons, Moten also does this in "The Case of Blackness"), since it is precisely the circumstance in which blackness finds itself that, Adorno would argue, ensures its continuation; art and philosophy, he says, "survive because the moment to realize [them] was missed."[65] Adorno's paradox is reminiscent of Wilderson's not so "easy grammatical join of art and liberation"—performance falls short precisely because it is an accompaniment to structural change and not necessary to it. For art to hit its target is for it to no longer *be* art. This predicament mirrors the one blackness is in, for blackness, too, cannot hope to ever coincide with itself because of the structural interventions of antiblackness and the processes that remove black people from the world. And yet much of hip hop aspires to a condition under which language, and the black culture that blossoms through it, becomes the realization of this

---

[65] Theodor Adorno, *Negative Dialectics*, trans. E.B. Ashton (New York: Continuum, 2007), 2–3. See also "Cultural Criticism and Society," in *Prisms* (Cambridge, MA: MIT, 1983), 17–34.

original coincidence and, in so doing, recovers its freedom and becomes something other than performance. This is what the flow *is*, after all, and the aspiration toward it illustrates how hip hop cuts across the nature of performance as such and in the process provides an analogy to black life that truly belongs to it. In other words, when hip hop hits its target, blackness per se, it, too, ceases to be performance and becomes something else in becoming itself.

Hip hop, then, *is* an historical performance of this ongoing subjective and social hermeneutics, a constant "break[ing] it down," so to speak, just as the history of black musical traditions and the critical preoccupations of afropessimism are expressions of the same *care*. Even though the world cannot ever return to a world in which there is no slave, it can also never reach a place in time at which what it means to be black, and perhaps even the possibility of its meaning nothing at all, can be permanently decided. Blackness, too, is something always still to be settled, and so contains within it the ever-present possibility of its becoming, along the way, something else entirely. This is more likely than not the case if we can bring ourselves to imagine the social-ontological death of "blackness" (and the afropessimist tradition that responds to it) as the symptom of a more authentic black free agency and of the diminishment of white power and antiblackness instead of *only* as the cruel effect of whiteness.

Afropessimism rightly prompts scholars to contend with the confrontation in hip hop between black performativity and black liberation and thus also to engage with the structural (and painful) basis of black nonexistence as it is made manifest in hip hop, but the degree to which blackness escapes this confrontation and cultivates itself in the turn toward itself is nevertheless rendered even more sharply (perhaps too obviously so?) in those moments when hip hop, and the blackness to which it attests, rather unapologetically delights in itself and in that very existence which elsewhere is structurally denied to it. Certainly one could count the playfulness of early hip hop as an example of this joyful resistance, alongside so many other examples throughout the life of the genre, including, for example, Outkast's "Player's Ball" (1994)—"I'm talking 'bout a black man heaven here"; the legendary, bitter-sweet nostalgia in the opening verse of Notorious BIG's "Juicy" (1994)—"It was all a dream/I used to read Word UP! magazine"; or Master P's "We Bout Dat" (2000), in which, even as the track acknowledges the systemic violence in which blackness is caught up, nevertheless emphasizes the rhythmic, almost universal, pleasure of an everyday black urban belonging—"We in the projects/livin' nigga/rollin' with my boys [...]." From this perspective, the joy of hip hop lies in its collective making of a blackened world and in the empowerment inherent in the counter-performance of blackness as such. As a result, even if we accept the allegations surrounding its end, black life is encouraged, not discouraged, because hip hop *was*, and if hip hop *can* be said to have ended, then this is because the moment to realize it was *not* missed.

Disclaimer.
"The views expressed in this chapter are the author's own and do not represent the views, politics, or positions of the US Department of Defense, Department of the Navy, or the US Naval War College"

BIBLIOGRAPHY

Adorno, Theodor. *Negative Dialectics*. Trans. E.B. Ashton. New York: Continuum, 2007.
———. "Cultural Criticism and Society." In *Prisms*. Cambridge, MA: MIT Press, 1983.
Butler, Judith. *Gender Trouble: Feminism and the Subversion of Identity*. New York: Routledge, 2002.
Deleuze, Gilles, and Felix Guattari. *A Thousand Plateaus*. Minneapolis: Minnesota University Press, 1987.
Dimitriadis, Greg. "Hip-Hop: From Live Performance to Mediated Narrative." In *That's the Joint: The Hip-Hop Studies Reader*. Eds. Murray Forman and Mark Anthony Neal. New York: Routledge, 2004.
Duinker, Ben and Denis Martin. "In Search of the Golden Age of Hip-Hip Sound (1986-1996)." *Empirical Musicology Review* 12.1-2 (2017): 80-100.
Dyson, Michael Eric. "The Culture of Hip-Hop." In *That's the Joint: The Hip-Hop Studies Reader*. Eds. Murray Forman and Mark Anthony Neal. New York: Routledge, 2004.
Gordon, Lewis. "Black Existence in Philosophy and Culture." *Diogenes* 59.3-4 (2014).
Heidegger, Martin. *Being and Time*. Trans. John Macquarrie and Edward Robinson. New York: Harper and Row, 1962.
Hartman, Saidiya. *Scenes of Subjection*. Oxford: Oxford University Press, 1997.

McKittrick, Katherine (and Sylvia Wynter). *Sylvia Wynter: On Being Human as Praxis*, ed. Katherine McKittrick, New York: Duke University Press, 2015.

Moten, Fred. "The Case of Blackness." *Criticism* 50.2 (2008).

————. *In the Break: The Aesthetics of the Black Radical Tradition*. Minneapolis: Minnesota University Press: 2003.

Neal, Mark Anthony. *That's the Joint: The Hip-Hop Studies Reader*. Eds. Murray Forman and Mark Anthony Neal New York: Routledge, 2004.

————. *What the Music Said: Black Popular Music and Black Public Culture*. New York: Routledge, 1999.

Saucier, P. Khalil, and Tryon P. Woods. "Hip Hop Studies in Black." *Journal of Popular Music Studies*. 26.2-3 (2014).

Sexton, Jared. *Amalgamation Schemes: Antiblackness and the Critique of Multiracialism*. Minneapolis: Minnesota University Press, 2008.

————, and Huey Copeland. "Raw Life: An Introduction." *Qui Parle* (2003).

————. "The Social Life of Social Death: On Afro-Pessimism and Black Optimism." *InTensions* 5 (2011).

Thomas, Greg. *Hip Hop Revolution in the Flesh: Power, Knowledge, and Pleasure in Lil' Kim's Lyricism*. New York: Palgrave Macmillan, 2009.

Weheliye, Alexander G. "'Feenin': Posthuman Voices in Contemporary Black Popular Music." *Social Text 71*. 20.2 (2002).

Wilderson, Frank. "Grammar and Ghosts: The Performative Limits of African Freedom." *Theatre Survey*. 50.1 (May 2009).

Transcultural Flow and the Problem of the Cipher

P. Khalil Saucier

As a teenager, the agile samples, staccato lines, and binding beats of Trenton, New Jersey's Poor Righteous Teachers kept my head-nodding. Yet, it wasn't until a few years later that the authoritative and punctual lyrics from the group's lead emcee, Wise Intelligent, started to impact my perception, recognition, and understanding of *this* world. The lyrical frames from which Wise Intelligent "dropped knowledge" provided my friends and I with a language to better grasp and give expression to the phenomenological and lived experiences of black people in the United States. As Wise suggests on the track "The Nation's Anthem," "The knowledge of the cipher/Is to enlighten you."[1] In other words, by taking part in hip hop culture, namely through a myriad of ciphers from b-boying, basement gatherings, and more, "the knowledge of the cipher" began to

---

[1] "The Nation's Anthem," Poor Righteous Teachers, *Pure Poverty*, Profile Records, 1991. The line "The knowledge of the cipher/Is to enlighten you" can also be heard in the music of "Allah and Justice," Brand Nubian, *In God We Trust*, Elektra Records, 1993.

P. K. Saucier (✉)
Department of Critical Black Studies, Bucknell University, Lewisburg, PA, USA
e-mail: pks008@bucknell.edu

P. K. Saucier (ed.), *Critical Essays on Hip Hop and the Study of Hip Hop*, https://doi.org/10.1007/978-3-031-80763-3_3

39

lay bare the structures of the Social. The haunting echoes of what was actually occurring in the city of Trenton, for example, provided me with an opening, a means to "do the knowledge" and to interrogate life in the United States. The sonic epistemology of the Poor Righteous Teachers that placed the significance of the cipher in addition to hip hop's transculturality, a term that I will explore further in the following sections, unsettled both my perceptions and my sensibilities about the world, disrupting and challenging my narrow and normative assumptions about the human and the social, more specifically. In other words, hip hop culture assisted me by providing the analytical tools necessary for understanding the incommensurability of black experiences.[2]

Despite "growing old in the game," my ethical commitment for "doing the knowledge" has not wavered, and as such my understanding of "the cipher" has gone through an analytical metamorphosis. Using an amended notion of the cipher, beyond a dialogical gathering, but an understanding and symbol found within hip hop culture, nonetheless, I have come to question and by extension disturb the epistemological grounds of hip hop ethnography and the identitarian and transcultural exceptionalism that continues to guide such a methodological practice.[3] In order to disturb the epistemological pretext of hip hop ethnography it is paramount that we take seriously the political ontology of blackness, that is, to rethink blackness, on the one hand, as a sign within the political economy of difference, and on the other hand, understand blackness as an expression of a worldmaking paradigm, what Caribbean philosopher Sylvia Wynter has called "monohumanism."[4] My aim in this chapter is to place emphasis on the latter which in turn calls for an ethical cynicism and teleological suspension of the analytic and agentic capacity of transcultural representations of difference within hip-hop. It is my belief that ethnography's fidelity to transculturalism mimics the earlier zeitgeist of multiculturalism and also militates against fully comprehending the reality that blackness is ontologically distinct. As I will explore, the black subject

---

[2] For a complete exploration concerning the false universality of the human and the social see, Moon-Kie Jung and João H. Costa Vargas, "More than and beyond racism: theoretical and political meditations on antiblackness," *Souls* 23.3–4 (2022): n.p.

[3] Also known to some as hiphopgraphy. For more on hiphopgraphy see, James G. Spady, "Mapping and Re-Membering Hip Hop History, Hiphopography and African Diasporic History." *Western Journal of Black Studies* 37.2 (2013): 126–157.

[4] Greg Thomas, "Wynter with Fanon in the FLN: The" Rights of Peoples" against the "Monohumanism" of 'Man'," *American Quarterly* 70.4 (2018): 857–865.

which is often central to what constitutes hip hop ethnography is a social cipher; that is, in the words of Tendayi Sithole, "The black subject is not a subject of distinction or difference; it is … the *subject of not* …."[5] In order to grasp incommensurability of black experiences, it is imperative that hip hop ethnographies, on the one hand, distinguish between race and racism and more so realize that antiblackness is not racism and, on the other hand, emphasize that the transculturalism of hip-hop signals more than identity politics, but also an ethically-oriented politics of identification. With this in mind, I ask the question, can the transcultural dimensions of hip hop allow us to undertake the study of a position, rather than of a transcultural identity in action? In other words, how do hip hop ethnographies understand transcultural blackness that is structurally and symbolically imposed? What essential insight has hip hop ethnography missed in its understanding of the racialized imaginary of "monohumanism?"

As such, I explore the problematic connection between a form of understanding structured by grammars of difference which further constitute and extend liberal humanism's horizon in lieu of a "Black Horizon," which "is not about an affirmation of black life but the necessary disavowal of black life as figure for the disavowal of all life that is beyond the grasp of modern ontology."[6] In other words, transcultural accounts evoke a multiracial and multicultural cipher of people, but at the expense of a form of being and sociality that refuses to be part of this world. As I will attempt to show, the utilization of transcultural flow is a means to disrupt the ahistorical narrative that hip hop culture is merely a North American cultural affair, a tale hamstrung by cultural essentialist notions of blackness. Therefore, my goal is to shed light on the general, but implicit grounds on which global hip hop studies often sits and its concern for the inclusion of the ethnographic "other," and not an ethical confrontation with the antiblackness of the world. In a sense, difference, illustrated by the complexity of hip hop practices globally, is instrumentalized in order to correct the linear path of history. In short, for all its efforts to delink the field's epistemology from dominant logic, global hip hop studies stays within the racial logics of modernity, a stance that is complicit, more specifically with monohumanism, not its perversion.

---

[5] Tendayi Sithole, Tendayi. *The black register* (New York: Polity, 2020), 7. Emphasis in the original.

[6] Farai Chipato and David Chandler, "The black horizon: Alterity and ontology in the Anthropocene," *Global Society* 37.2 (2023): 167.

Voice Lessons

Although many scholars argued for its methodological inclusion, for years, hip hop studies ignored ethnography as a robust and informative methodology.[7] On the one hand, ethnography was a means to exceed the textual trends dominant in hip hop studies.[8] On the other hand, ethnography was a means and method to transcend what Michael Jefferies calls "outdated and racialized hip-hop essentialism."[9] Such wheedling led many global hip hop scholars interested in transculturalism to take up ethnography as a means to give voice to those being studied.

Echoing earlier observations, scholar Kevin Holt has suggested that "the very scholars working to give voice to hip-hop communities in some ways centralize methodologies that perpetuate their voicelessness."[10] Holt implies that hip hop studies would benefit from more ethnographic research for scholars too often "speak *for* hip-hoppers"[11] rather than allowing for the true "subjectivity of hip-hoppers"[12] to be expressed. Arguably, hip hop ethnography is the preferred medium for accessing the "voices from within the veil" whether in the US or abroad.[13] Preferred because it allows researchers to engage with the complexity and nuance of lived experiences to describe how lives are actually lived, rather than reduce them to so-called theoretical abstractions that are all too often seen as totalizing propositions.

While there is something to be said about the discursive practice of speaking *for* others, I am not entirely convinced that more ethnography is or would be the antidote. Simply "listening to" participants is an uncritical endeavor in itself, for it suggests that hip hoppers, in this case, can self-evidently draft their own lived experiences, interests, and more. In other

[7] See, for example, Kwame Anthony Harrison, "Hip-hop and racial identification: an (auto)ethnographic perspective" in *The Cambridge Companion to Hip-Hop*, ed. Justin A. Williams (Cambridge: Cambridge University Press, 2015), 152–167.

[8] See, for example, Greg Dimitriadis, "Framing hip hop: New methodologies for new times," *Urban Education* 50.1 (2015): 31–51.

[9] Michael P. Jeffries, "Hip-hop Urbanism Old and New," *International Journal of Urban and Regional Research* 38.2 (2014): 707.

[10] Kevin C. Holt, "Emcee Ethnographies: A Brief Sketch of US Hip-Hop Ethnography," (2019): 11.

[11] Holt, "Emcee Ethnographies," 11.

[12] Holt, "Emcee Ethnographies," 19.

[13] (DuBois 1999).

words, while there is abundant concern about the ideological commit-
ments and stances of the scholars, there is little to no concern for the ways
in which hip hoppers frame their phenomenological experiences, suggesting that they do not have a normative or non-ideological understanding of
their being in the world.[14] Arguably, ethnographies are a performative
medium for scholars to incorporate the silenced and otherwise repressed
voices of the global hip hop nation.[15] The voice that speaks for itself is
understood as a more effective instrument and epistemically salient than
the so-called authority of the scholar, producing an intimacy of sound and
audibility that speaks rather than represents. However, with just the voice,
more often than not, the structural position of the practitioner, and for my
concerns the blackness of the practitioner, is redacted allowing interested
and empathetic parties to bond. That which is descriptively and ideologi-
cally hegemonic (e.g., the discourse of identity) gets drowned out by hip
hop's transcultural bond and the voice of the hip hopper.

Case in point, more often than not, hip hop ethnographies, in some
ways, embrace blackness as being a part of the world, albeit simply discon-
nected and marginalized, rather than illustrative of its incommensurability
and aporetic conflict with the logic of racial affirmation and representation. In other words, blackness is nothing more than an identity that is
embraced and accomplished. Little is done to mark a distinction between
black racial identity and blackness. That is, to think beyond race as merely
identity and as something rooted in violence not classification; a political
ontology trapped in a modern dialectic of recognition.

Starting from Tricia Rose's seminal text *Black Noise: Rap Music and
Black Culture in Contemporary America*, to similarly inspired works of
today, hip hop ethnographies are interested in connecting the discursive,
digital, and material terrain of hip hop culture to the ways in which its
participants refuse and/or resist the authority of the state and other

[14] This tension between speaking for and listening to is richly developed in Spivak, Gayatri
Chakravorty. "Can the subaltern speak?" in Peter J. Cain and Mark Harrison, eds.
Imperialism: critical concepts in historical studies. Vol. 3. 171–219, (New York: Taylor &
Francis, 2004).

[15] See, Awad Ibrahim, "Arab Spring, favelas, borders, and the artistic transnational migration: Toward a curriculum for a global hip-hop nation," in Elana Toukan, Rubèn
A. Gaztambide-Fernandez, and Sardar M. Anwaruddin, eds. *Curriculum of Global Migration
and Transnationalism*, 103–111, (New York: Routledge, 2020).

oppressive entities.[16] To be fair, hip hop ethnographies often deploy "blackness" as a double narrative and not a single discourse.[17] First, blackness is understood to be an incidental outcome of marginalization, a product of systemic racism played out in the streets, the favela, shantytown, etc.[18] Second, blackness, following Achille Mbembe, is "a declaration of identity."[19] Hip hop ethnographies see an entanglement between the two, but place emphasis on the latter in order to buck the trends that are understood to be non-creative and anti-agentic; that is to move beyond critique, contradiction and the negative itself and build, generate, and produce.

For example, Bryce Henson extends this observation in his fascinating book *Emergent Quilombos*. Henson makes an interesting claim that "the Bahian hip-hop movement nourishes, maintains, and retools the quilombo (maroon community) blueprint to assert Black life and diasporic cultures in and against contemporary Brazil."[20] As he mentions "Bahian hip-hop carries … [the] baton" of the Brazilian black radical tradition, while utilizing Omi and Winant in order to set the stage for arguing that blackness is not static, but fluid and multiple. For him "the Bahian hip-hop movement exposes the multiple Blacknesses of Brazil."[21] Henson presents it as "an alternative to the prevailing three types of Blackness that occupy the Brazilian imaginary; abject Blackness, folklore Blackness, and mixed Blackness."[22] In parsing out blackness, largely as an identity, Henson

---

[16] Tricia Rose, *Black Noise: Rap music and Black cultural resistance in contemporary American popular culture* (Middletown: Wesleyan University, 1994). My early work on hip hop culture unfortunately only celebrates hip hop's confrontation with authority, see P. Khalil Saucier, ed. *Native Tongues: An African Hip Hop Reader,* (Trenton: Africa World Press, 2011); P. Khalil Saucier, "Continental drift: the politics and poetics of African hip hop," In *Sounds and the City: Popular Music, Place, and Globalization*, 196–208, (London: Palgrave Macmillan UK, 2014); and P. Khalil Saucier and Kumarini Silva, "Keeping it real in the global south: Hip-hop comes to Sri Lanka," *Critical Sociology* 40, no. 2 (2014): 295–300.

[17] Achille Mbembe, *Critique of black reason* (Durham: Duke University Press, 2017), 28.

[18] See, for example, Marcos Morgado, "Translocal Hip Hop Aesthetics: Contemporary Performances in Brazilian Hip Hop." *Global Hiphopography*. Cham: Springer International Publishing, 2023. 273–298; Marcyliena Morgan, *Hip-Hop en Français: An Exploration of Hip-Hop Culture in the Francophone World*. Rowman & Littlefield, 2020; Halifu Osumare, "Keeping it Real: Race, Class, and Youth Connections Through Hip-Hop in the US & Brazil," *Humboldt Journal of Social Relations* 37 (2015): 6–18.

[19] Mbembe, *Critique of black reason*, 28.

[20] Bryce Henson, *Emergent Quilombos: Black Life and Hip-Hop in Brazil* (Austin: University of Texas Press, 2023), 3.

[21] Henson, *Emergent Quilombos*, 9.

[22] Henson, *Emergent Quilombos*, 9.

rightfully connects to the human and non-human divide, an important categorical distinction which so many hip hop scholars neglect and sees hip hop in Brazil as a "refuge."[23] In providing a refuge from the political chaos of Brazil, Henson unhinges identity from the nation and orients it toward a global hip hop nation with an alternative form of citizenship. In doing so, he is able to claim that hip hop in Brazil "refuses mixed and folkloric Blackness ... [for they] reduce race to culture, heritage, and biology."[24] Henson "sees abject Blackness," what could be construed as the "the ledge," "as a radical site of possibility and transformation by attempting to claim other meanings for those marked as nonnormative, noncitizen, and nonhuman."[25] Henson, rightfully puts pressure on the folkloric and mixed/hybrid forms of identity that are often identified in hip hop ethnographies, but does so with a lack of emphasis on the structural, leaving open the door for identity and the formation of an imagined hip hop community, a reiteration of human subjectivity that claims its own kind of interiority; a kind of "radical" refurbishing of human interiority.

By placing emphasis on blackness as identity most ethnographic accounts address the performative which alleviate suggested and historical forms of racial essentialism and intra- and inter-racial conflict once and for all—a maneuver, which I intended to explore in brief and schematically, as an attempt to extricate itself from the antagonism that is blackness. Given this conflation, I believe that, if we are ethically going to "do the knowledge" in hip hop studies, there is a need to work from the idea that blackness, while an identity in action, is also a position that is constitutive of both the social and the human. Returning to the idea of the social cipher, the social cipher that is blackness in the modern world is a semiotic figure that helps organize and authorize dispossession, displacement, and more. In other words, the political economy of difference, that which makes up the transcultural, is no doubt a phenomenological reality, but most studies that emphasis this reality do so at the expense of the irresolvable difference of antiblackness. They provide slices of everyday life that highlight the fluidity and complexity of blackness and in doing so highlight various forms of agency and cultural authorization: the ways in which their racial identity, not their *being* in the world, is predicated upon a transcultural refusal and how this refusal operates in everyday encounters to reaffirm

---

[23] Henson, *Emergent Quilombos,* 12.
[24] Henson, *Emergent Quilombos,* 13.
[25] Henson, *Emergent Quilombos,* 13.

their existence. Rather than misconstrue or oversimplify blackness as a cultural identity, what happens when hip hop ethnographies that prioritize the transcultural set aside the trappings of modernity's dialectic of recognition, for the very thing that DuBois observed binds "the children of Africa … [in] a common disaster"?[26]

Connected to this argument is how the transcultural has little regard for the social and the human and by extension operates as an alibi for dismissing the structural position of blackness. Transcultural flow as it relates to hip hop is best exemplified by the idea or "imagined community" of the global hip hop nation. For example, in Sujatha Fernandes's *Close to the Edge* Fernandes writes, "The Hip Hop Nation as a transnational space of mutual learning and exchange may not have been a concrete reality. But the transient alliances that hip hoppers imagined across boundaries of class, race, and nation gave them the resources and the platform they needed to tell their stories and provided the grounds for their locally based political actions."[27] Hip hop culture, in this sense, is a unifying phenomenon that bucks nation, ethnicity, and more. From Napoli to the Bronx, Stockholm to Marrakech hip hop, with its various practices, crosses boundaries and borders, connecting the residents and denizens of these places. It is an active medium that can bring discontented northern Arabs of Algeria together with those occupying the favelas of Brazil. As a dialogical global force, hip hop's transnationalism is post-facto transcultural.

For some time now, the transcultural functionality of hip hop that produces a collective identity has been captured in the metaphor phenomenological descriptor, flow. Given that flow is a significant metaphor within hip hop studies, especially after Tricia Rose's *Black Noise*, the ur-text of hip hop studies, explored it as a fundamental agentic characteristic of hip hop along with layering and rupture. Hip hop's transcultural flows are at once linguistic, spatial, temporal, epistemological, and axiological.[28] Flow helps

---

[26] W.E.B DuBois, *Dusk of Dawn: The Autobiography of W.E.B. DuBois* (New York: Harcourt 1940), 116.

[27] Sujatha Fernandes, *Close to the Edge: In search of the global hip hop generation* (New York: Verso Books, 2011), 4.

[28] See, for example, Sammy Alim, H. and Alistair Pennycook. *Global linguistic flows* (Taylor & Francis, 2008); Arjun Appadurai, *Modernity at large: Cultural dimensions of globalization* (Minneapolis: U of Minnesota Press, 1996); Ibrahim, "Arab Spring, favelas, borders, and the artistic transnational migration," 103–111; Alastair Pennycook, *Global Englishes and Transcultural Flows* (New York: Routledge, 2006); James G. Spady, Samir Meghelli, and H. Samy Alim, *Tha Global Cipha: Hip Hop Culture and Consciousness* (Philadelphia: Black

construct a sense of relationality and a shared sociality, comforting hip hop scholars because the relationship between black social death (i.e., the social cipher) and hip hop subjectivity is one of perceived mutuality. It, therefore, seems less parasitic knowing that there is a "communal bond" rather than a violent dependency on black social and physical death. This sort of posturing of an undifferentiated sociality further buoys hip hop studies' desire for and investment in hip hop's capacity to rupture oppressive metaphysics. Yet, there is a failure to acknowledge that such theorizations of what Halifu Osumare calls "connective marginalities"[29] emerge from and are signified by the violent history of antiblack terror, urban decay, hyper concentration, and more.

For example, one space that connects, prioritizes, and regards the transcultural qualities of hip hop is Italy. Over the years, scholars have framed hip hop as one of many racial projects that offers black youth in Italy, a performance medium for channeling stored desires and more. Given that Italy is a place, as Camille Hawthorne suggests, where "Blackness and Black people are marked as the most extreme symbols of national nonbelonging," the elements of hip hop are understood to be impactful practices of self-production.[30] Scholars such as Scarparo and Stevenson understand hip hop as giving "voice to marginal languages and perspectives which counter colonial and neo-colonial hegemonies ... provide a parallel means of self-representation which reinterprets marginality and challenges dominant discourses and narratives."[31] Similarly Dolasinski understands hip hop as providing a space where Italian youth accomplish hybrid identities, maintaining proximity to the world. As a transcultural instrument, hip hop provides the resources to construct/fabulate "in between identities that are relatable to, and representative of, Italy's increasingly diverse youth generation."[32] Hip hop, in this instance, is a

History Museum Press, 2006); Quetin Williams and Jaspal Naveel Singh, "Introduction: Hip Hop's Here, There... and Everywhere—An Introduction to Global Hiphopography," in Quetin Williams and Jaspal Naveel Singh, eds. *Global hiphopography*. 1–25. (London: Palgrave Macmillan, 2023).

[29] Halifu Osumare, *The Africanist aesthetic in global hip-hop: Power moves* (New York: Palgrave Macmillan, 2016).

[30] Camilla Hawthorne, *Contesting race and citizenship: youth politics in the Black Mediterranean* (Ithaca: Cornell University Press, 2022), 41.

[31] Susanna, Scarparo and Mathias Sutherland Stevenson, "Transcultural flows and marginality: reggae and hip hop in Sardinia," *Modern Italy* 25.2 (2020): 209.

[32] Lisa Dolasinski, "'In Between' Ethnic Heritage and Italian Identity: The Global Hip-Hop of Mahmood and Ghali," *The Italianist* 42.1 (2022): 121.

means to challenge national homogeneity and illustrate that Italy is much more than what the political register suggests. While these studies are not ethnographic in nature, they no doubt model what hip hop ethnographies too often do, that is, re-create and overemphasize the agentic possibility embedded in the culture with little attention to philosophical tenets of the hip hopper.[33]

Susanna Scarparo and Mathais Sutherland Stevenson directly frame Italian hip hop as "a counter hegemonic transcultural force."[34] Inspired by Fernanod Ortiz, Scarparo and Stevenson, place great analytic value on the term "transculturation" highlighting that "[t]he prefix *trans* can be understood to denote movement, or a process of moving across or beyond, but also a process of cultural *transferal* and *transformation*."[35] Hip hop, along with reggae, two black cultural imports, is a means to transform one's subjectivity. Inspired by Antonio Gramsci, Stuart Hall, and others they point out that certain emcees, for example, are *in* the world, but not *of* the world.[36] In doing so, they prefer descriptors of marginalization such as "multidimensional marginality (207)" or Halifu Osumare's notion of "connective marginalities."[37] In deploying marginalities, it allows scholars to flatten the political reality of some versus others and find agency and self-possession; rather than blacken their understanding and think about blackness as a violently imposed position that begets marginality, dispossession, and ultimately non-being. In short, blackness is reinstated as an aesthetic accoutrement for accomplishing a transcultural identity.

Transcultural blackness within hip hop ethnography becomes a cultural identity that is temporally and spatially situated and lends itself to identitarian heterogeneity, and consequently, greater socio-cultural complexity that supposedly only ethnography paired with hip hop texts can capture. Hip hop allows for a subjective negotiation, a performance of another way of being in the world. It is my contention that racial performances, often read ethnographically as acts of refusal, must always be calibrated to the ontological coherence of society. The ontological position creates the

---

[33] See Dimitriadis, "Framing hip hop," 31–51.
[34] Scarparo and Stevenson, "Transcultural flows and marginality," 200.
[35] Scarparo and Stevenson, "Transcultural flows and marginality,"199.
[36] Scarparo and Stevenson, "Transcultural flows and marginality," 201.
[37] Susanna Scarparo, and Mathias Sutherland Stevenson, *Reggae and Hip Hop in southern Italy: Politics, languages, and multiple marginalities* (Cham, Switzerland: Springer, 2018), 6. See also, Osumare, *The Africanist aesthetic in global hip-hop*.

conditions for the discursive and symbolic, not the reverse. Race is not first and foremost performative. Rather, race is performative after being ontologically positioned. Italy, in this case, becomes a flat plane and hip hop helps facilitate a secondary (re)unification, the *Risorgimento 2.0*. In other words, blackness is not enlisted for its analytic value, but instead to generate possibilities for becoming; the transcultural is not an "ontological insurrection," but simply a transformation of what it means to be Italian, while sublating antiblackness.[38] To quote theorist Zallaou there is "too much becoming … and not enough being (what objects are)."[39] If race, in this instance is more than racism, scholars do not have to wallow in the ethical dilemmas that attending to antiblackness would present. They can attend to social life in the midst of wayward and retrograde nationalism, xenophobia, urban decay, migrant crisis, police brutality, and the like without coming to terms with the social cipher and the "monohumanism" that structures it. New or old, "identity" is epiphenomenal to the slaveholding enterprise. While I do not deny the multiplicity of black subjectivity and the diversity of black experience throughout the African diaspora, I think it is imperative to place under analytic pressure the antiblack schema underwriting hip hop ethnography and hip hop studies more generally and the inviolable willingness to sacrifice black interests for "monohumanism," transcendental empiricism, and ethnographic nuance. That is, instead of thinking of blackness solely from the grounds that it is in the world and not of it, I would like to point out that the social cipher is of course in the world and, while it can be debated if it is not of the world, it most importantly is not *for* it.[40]

The way I see it, placing a premium on *transcultural flow* and on the cipher in the normative sense, may say something about the shared scales of oppression of global youth, but it also generates profound analytical blind spots that undermine black freedom and self-possession. As such, it is important that we trace the limits of, and explicitly depart from hip hop ethnography's logic, and explore the antagonism of blackness beyond transcultural identity. In doing so, I suggest, we need to rethink our

[38] Marquis Bey, *The Problem of the Negro as a Problem for Gender* (Minneapolis: University of Minnesota Press, 2020), 78.

[39] Zahi Zalloua, *Being Posthuman: Ontologies of the Future* (London: Bloomsbury, 2021), 113.

[40] Andrew Culp, *Dark Deleuze* (Minneapolis: University of Minnesota Press, 2016), 8.

analytical orientation, place emphasis on the social cipher that chooses not to fully mimic western ways of being and shift away from the logic of hip hop scholasticism that reproduces the terms of order that prohibit hip hop studies from ethically confronting antiblackness.[41]

HACKING THE CIPHER

Hip hop ciphers abound. There is the emcee cipher, the dance cipher, radio cipher to name only a few. For Samy Alim the cipher is the ultimate expression of the hip hop community; an innovative expressive and kinetic space intelligible to its practitioners, but not outsiders.[42] Relatedly, for Imani Perry, the cipher is "a conceptual space in which heightened consciousness exists" and where "alternative ethos and subjectivity" are formed."[43] This exclusionary manifestation of consciousness/epistemology has long roots in annals of black history and life; located in secular black folk songs, black literary traditions from Richard Wright to Amiri Barka, to five percenter ideology exhibited in Wu Tang.[44] According to Jeff Chang, "In the cipher, hip-hop's vitality is reaffirmed, its participants recommit to its primacy, and the culture transforms itself."[45]

As I stated many years ago, a cipher can tell us much about the relationship between poetic expression and political composition, but the social cipher of blackness is also an urgent hermeneutic, something that allows us to think of social death, that is in excess of the protocols of ethnography.[46] According to the Cambridge Dictionary, it defines two of the multiple definitions for cipher as a noun (person) that "a person or group of people without power, but used by others for their own purposes, or

---

[41] The argument that there is an unethical alignment between the problem and its critics, also the problem, is further elaborated in my work with Tryon P. Woods.

[42] Samy H. Alim, *Roc the mic right: The language of hip hop culture* (New York: Routledge, 2006).

[43] Imani Perry, *Prophets of the hood: Politics and poetics in hip hop* (Durham: Duke University Press, 2004), 107–108.

[44] For secular folk songs see, Patrick S. Bernard, "A" Cipher Language"," *African American Review* 52.2 (2019): 121–142. For black literary traditions see James Braxton Peterson, "A Cipher of the Underground in Black Literary Culture," *The Hip-Hop Underground and African American Culture: Beneath the Surface*. 83–99. (New York: Palgrave Macmillan, 2014).

[45] Jeff Chang, ed. *Total chaos: The art and aesthetics of hip-hop* (New York: Civitas Books, 2006), 4.

[46] Saucier, "Continental drift," 196–208.

someone who is not important"[47] and "a zero, or a person or thing that has no value or importance." In order to deploy the cipher as an urgent hermeneutic, it is important to place emphasis on the latter which in turn provides a paradigmatic lens from which to understand the continuous enunciation of violence that continues to sustain the regime of immanent distinction. In addition, my comments should not be taken as the de-animation of Black social life in Europe, but rather as an exploration of the libidinal and psychic function of transcultural blackness within the discursive terrain of the global imaginary. Put differently, prioritizing the "voice" of hip hop practitioners suffers, in my estimation, from an agentic extravagance. The quest for a differentiated wholeness obscures the social cipher that could fundamentally disrupt the unity of the whole and this world. In being a part of the global hip hop community, many hip hop ethnographies risk a form of emancipatory delusion, a "desire for a sublime historicity that, paradoxically, ends up denying time and alterity."[48] The metalanguage deployed fails to account for the ontological cleft, the fundamental antagonism that disrupts the linearity and finitude of understanding. Hip hop ethnography turns away from universality of the social cipher to identity betraying freedom and community. Betraying the culture.[49]

To clarify, instead of imbibing in the normative currency of cipher, I want to offer the idea, in some ways inspired by early hip hop, such as the Poor Righteous Teachers, that blackness is a social cipher, as a sign of political ontology; a cryptogram of nothingness. Denise Ferreira da Silva, in "Hacking the Subject," suggests that "the cypher means at once: (a) the disappearance of value (nullification); (b) the absence of value (nothingness); (c) beyond any means of or measuring (excess); and, more importantly, (d) the plenum (virtuality, as a possible new origin or beginning) (31)." At issue is the generative yield of the cipher as a place of transcultural flow on the one hand *or* as a manifestation of all the fantasies, fears, and desires of society on the other hand. This refiguring of the cipher is an especially important insight from black study that hip hop ethnography has failed to take seriously. However, while ethnography, intentionally or

[47] "Cipher," *Cambridge Dictionary*, Accessed June 2, 2024 https://dictionary.cambridge. org/us/dictionary/english/cipher

[48] David Marriott, "On Crystallization," *Critical Times* 4, no. 2 (2021): 210.

[49] See Jim Vernon, *Sampling, biting, and the postmodern subversion of hip hop* (Cham, Switzerland; Palgrave Macmillan, 2021).

unintentionally, works within this framework of "Who and What am I?" it often sidesteps the "what" and by extension evacuates the meaning and import of blackness by conflating it with black identity. Such a maneuver allows for ethnographic approaches to overvalue the "who" which is made up of what people think, say, and do (i.e., culture) and thereby overemphasize a presumed subjectivity. Eliminating or neglecting "what one is" presupposes an ontological equality and does not account for the funk of living as a social cipher. This argument is partially extended in *Necessarily Black: Cape Verdean Youth, Hip-Hop Culture, and a Critique of Identity* (2015). *Necessarily Black* was my attempt to present identity always lived in the plural, but always structured by the singularity of blackness as negativity. The plurality of identities required mooring to a particular structural position. As a result, it does not contest the grounds from which blackness is constructed (although many emcees do in fact contest); instead, it glosses over this important social fact, the ontological significance of blackness, in order to write subjectivity into existence. To *be* black is much different than to *accomplish* a black identity.[50] In order to illustrate my concerns, I turn to one African diasporic example as a means to illustrate the aforementioned concerns.

Transcultural Blackness in India

Although I am not an expert on Indian popular culture, politics, or anything related to India for that matter, I turn to two examples of hip hop ethnography in India because: (1) they offer the most robust transcultural accounts to date; and (2) they focus on Africans in diaspora, one of my areas of specialty. The two scholars that I engage in this section, Ethiraj Gabriel Dattatreyan and Jaspal Naveel Singh overlap in their ethnographic approaches.[51] Both prioritize voice and how said voices can co-create transcultural products such as ethnographic films and digital spaces. In addition, both echo earlier calls for scholars to use ethnography as a means to access the interior of hip hop culture and its practitioners. Once again,

---

[50] This is a distinction, for example, that can be found in "Meditate," Earthgang, *Rags*, 2017, Interscope and "The Story of OJ Story," Jay Z, *4:44*, 2017, Roc Nation.

[51] Ethiraj Gabriel Dattatreyan, *The Globally Familiar: Digital Hip Hop, Masculinity, and Urban Space in Delhi* (Durham: Duke University Press, 2020). Jaspal Naveel Singh, *Transcultural voices: Narrating hip hop culture in complex Delhi* (Bristol: Multilingual Matters, 2021).

ethnography is understood to be ultimately a generative and productive methodology for accessing authentic accounts of participants.

In discussing the making of the film *Cry Out Loud*, thoughts further elaborated in his preoccupying book *The Globally Familiar: Digital Hip Hop, Masculinity, and Urban Space in Delhi*, Dattatreyan explicitly connects the idea of hip hop to ethnography, particularly the importance of "collaborative ethnographic filmmaking,"[52] as a means to illustrate the racial logics at play amongst Somali refugees in Satpula Delhi. More so, and in fact, Dattatreyan states that "the cipha … [is] an ethos that translated into a working model for collaboration."[53] As he points out in his book the hip hop cipha lends itself to "self-making projects" and a "shared anthropology."[54] Dattatreyan enthusiastically points out that one of his interlocutors proclaimed that "Ethnography is the fifth element!"[55] Similarly, Singh claims that his ethnographic work "is hip hop itself."[56]

Interestingly, Dattatreyan mobilizes a normative understanding of the cipher, emphasizing the collaborative spontaneity and social synergy of such a spatial and temporal gathering. The cipher, as a collaborative event, flattens power dynamics by which the ethnographer displaces their perceived power, self-reflexivity par excellence. The co-creationing it is assumed, affords an accurate reading of the power dynamics at play in Delhi between Somali youth and locals. In this formulation, hip hop is not an 'object' of study but rather an ethnographic opening by which to engage with concerns, dreams, and experiences of its practitioners."[57] If done well, meaning that it is reflexive and sincere, ethnographic knowledge production is understood to be transformative. While both scholars are wary of "speaking for" their interlocutors and simultaneously heedful of the decadents of ethnography, doing so does not *ipso facto* transform the paradigmatic frame.

Singh, for example, is committed to "anti-essentialist epistemology" of which ethnography is his preferred tool.[58] Yet the emphasis on difference and pluralism not only uncovers what we already know, that is cultural

---

[52] Ethiraj Gabriel Dattatreyan, "Critical hip-hop cinema: Racial logics and ethnographic ciphas in Delhi," *Wide Screen* 7, no. 1 (2018): 6.

[53] Dattatreyan, "Critical hip-hop cinema," 17.

[54] Dattatreyan, *The Globally Familiar*, 14.

[55] Dattatreyan, "Critical hip-hop cinema," 19.

[56] Singh, *Transcultural voices*, 28.

[57] Dattatreyan, "Critical hip-hop cinema," 14.

[58] Singh, *Transcultural voices*, 30.

identity is infinite and unbound, but it is not so much "anti-essentialist" as it is a pretext for (not ethically) confronting that which structures the social cipher in the first place. If antiblackness is paradigmatic who is to say ethnographic collaboration gets to the heart of the problem? For instance, Singh suggests that "voice" is social, yet he never questions what is constitutive of the social.[59] Are we to assume that those who eventually come to voice will always speak against the normative constraints of the social and the "Monohumanist symbolically encoded configuration" that bolsters it.[60] The social is never up for discussion. Relatedly, Singh suggests that "The interactive genre of storytelling, oral narrative, and small stories," of which I presume ethnography is included "can be regarded as an affordance that allows speakers to put forward complex orchestrations of polyphony."[61] In short, he sees "narrative as a social practice" but, once again, does little to unpack the social despite his use of affordance which suggests that such actions are based on the design of the environment, an action possibility formed by the relationship between an agent and the social.[62] Embedded in narrative are the fundamental means, of which Singh includes stance taking and sampling, by which participants create a voice for themselves, "their own voice." Singh notes "interactants take stances towards other interactants and towards emerging topics" which is skillfully paired with a "formula of appropriation."[63] It is in the realm of sampling and appropriation, where the connection between transculturation and hip hop are most productive for developing subjectivity or what Singh calls "a postcolonial sense of identity … [where] narrators control which voices they appropriate and how they use these appropriations appropriately."[64] By bringing together a polyphony of sound, lyrics, and voices and by selectively choosing which to deploy, "interactants" begin to break from the racial essentialism that haunts them.

Singh furthers his commitment to not "speaking for" and the transformative possibilities in developing a transcultural voice, by stating that

[59] Singh, *Transcultural voices*, 34–37.

[60] Sylvia Wynter and Katherine McKittrick, "Unparalleled catastrophe for our species? Or, to give humanness a different future: Conversations," in Katherine McKittrick, ed. *Sylvia Wynter: On being human as praxis* (Durham: Duke University Press, 2015), 11.

[61] Singh, *Transcultural voices*, 46.

[62] See, for example, J.J. Gibson, "The theory of affordances," in *Perceiving, acting, and knowing* R. Shaw and J. Bransford, eds. 67–82. Hillsdale: Lawrence Erlbaum, 1977.

[63] Singh, *Transcultural voices*, 51 and 58.

[64] Singh, *Transcultural voices*, 58.

"instead of trying to determine 'the' meaning of a voice or 'the' identity of an author," it is more constructive to see how they "make voices meaningful in narratives."[65] This meaning-making practice is temporal and simultaneously spatial, in creating a transcultural voice one begins to develop the tools, taking from Mignolo and others, a form of "border thinking."[66] Developing a voice begets a form of consciousness. In hip hop argot Singh calls this process "overstandin" which "[r]ather than being encoded in the body or in the embodied practices of languages, overstandin is an affective stance that emerges in one's reflective encounter with one's own mind."[67] Dattatreyan co-signs Singh's observations by placing emphasis on the "cipha" as a dialogical space where hip hop practitioners can "take up a critical and reflexive position about their experiences in and of Delhi."[68] Yet, with so much emphasis on "overstandin" and the dialogics of the "cipha," the labile threshold between both and what Sylvia Wynters calls the "politics of being" is overlooked.[69] This maneuver is similar to the paraontological turn in black studies that seeks to transcend the violence of blackness' formative and current constitution, yet does little to refuse "functions to reinscribe the violence of ontology from which it seeks to flee."[70] "Overstadin," in this sense, bucks the racial logics for the affective, linguistic, and embodied, along with the sensuous and immanent attributes of hip hop. Following Axelle Karera's useful insight around the vexed relationship between ontology and paraontology within black studies, "the task is to discern the unenclosed links between the structures and performances of black refusal(s) on the one hand, and the conceptual systems they wish to abandon on the other. For, insofar as

[65] Singh, *Transcultural voices*, 59.
[66] Singh, *Transcultural voices*, 233.
[67] Singh, *Transcultural voices*, 234.
[68] Dattatreyan, "Critical hip-hop cinema," 6.
[69] Sylvia Wynter, "Unsettling the coloniality of being/power/truth/freedom: Towards the human, after man, its overrepresentation—An argument," *CR: The new centennial review* 3.3 (2003): 319.
[70] Axelle Karera, "Paraontology: interruption, inheritance, or a debt one often regrets," *Critical Philosophy of Race* 10.2 (2022): 162. Examples of the paraontological turn include, but are not limited to, Margo Natalie Crawford, *Black Post-Blackness: The Black Arts Movement and Twenty-First-Century Aesthetics* (Champaign: University of Illinois Press, 2017); William David Hart, *The Blackness of Black: Key Concepts in Critical Discourse* (Lanham: Rowman & Littlefield, 2020); Ronald Judy, *Sentient flesh: Thinking in disorder, poièsis in black* (Durham: Duke University Press, 2020); Fred Moten, "The case of blackness," *Criticism* 50.2 (2008): 177–218.

both are linked by degrees of (*unwanted*) inheritance."[71] This "unwanted inheritance" is the hegemony of identity, subjective ready-mades available for (re)presenting humanity in all their transcultural glory.

While following the aesthetic conventions of hip hop scholarship, affirming the idea that hip hop as always already subversive, Dattatreyan does deploy the language of antiblackness, but not as a paradigm. Rather, it is merely a proxy for racism. As he states, the "cipha" also conditions "ways of seeing and representing Delhi as a place where anti-Blackness circulates and makes visible a complex political economy of difference."[72] According to Jared Sexton, "anti-blackness is not … simply an uncommonly pernicious racist ideology or even a uniquely injurious racist practice … it is, more fundamentally, an unconscious cultural structure, a grammar, a *weltanschauung*, a metaphysics that lives on well after, and despite, the destruction of metaphysics."[73] In following Sexton and others, my contention is rooted in how these experiences are framed. More specifically, do Somali youth in Delhi frame the world through the idea that race constitutes racism or the reverse? Or, what happens when the dialogical approach is already framed by antiblackness? If this is the case, no amount of "co-constituting a narrative" will change the way one sees and understands power.[74] How are ethics played out when co-creators conflate, for example, racism with antiblackness? If a "cipha" creates space for reflection and the reflection is paradigmatically grounded, what is the value in ethnography or any hiphopgraphy for that matter?

For example, core to his ethnographic approach as a mechanism for making "voicing possible" is an element of participatory documentary. That is, Dattatreyan allowed some Somali youth to document and capture their lives as they were influenced by hip hop culture. Providing cameras and sound equipment is understood to provide the means of authentic reflexivity, for both participant and ethnographer. Again, ethnography as a co-creation is central to the argument. Therefore, cameras in the hands of Somali youth is one of the ways by which Dattatreyan helps "overstand" and decolonize the western gaze; a means for interactants to have access to writing their own script. Yet, doing so is a double-edged sword for who is to say that the participating youth will carve out a space for themselves

---

[71] Karera, "Paraontology," 180 emphasis added.
[72] Dattatreyan, "Critical hip-hop cinema," 8.
[73] Jared Sexton, "Affirmation in the Dark," *The Comparatist* 43 (2019): 102.
[74] Dattatreyan, "Critical hip-hop cinema," 21.

within the system of ontological purgation and think beyond the hegemony of antiblackness and the politics of being? As Fanon warns, "And so it is not I who make a meaning for myself, but it is the meaning that was already there, pre-existing, waiting for me."[75] Therefore, it stands, for instance, that "voicing" might be what the late Lindon Barrett might call "the conceptual impossibility."[76] It is as if hip hop ethnography adheres to a trite reading of Fanon in proving dominant narratives wrong and thus (re)uniting humanity pulled apart, yet connected, by hip hop. That is, they misread Frantz Fanon's declaration "to make myself known" as righting the negation of subjectivity, finding and documenting the lost voices of hip hop practitioners.[77] Ethnographies premature declaration and embrace of identity qua voice. A voice may disrupt what is being said, but the structure of conversation remains, camouflaging the depth of the void of blackness.

The perception that race begets racism plays out in the ways Dattatreyan makes Somali youth experiences in Delhi intelligible, suggesting that symbolic violence, that is Africans construed as a race of savages and cannibals begets physical violence.[78] One example of violence that Dattatreyan discloses is that at one point while he and his co-creators were shooting *Cry Out Loud*, African students were targeted by local Delhi residents simply as antiblackness without explanation. Interestingly, Dattatreyan understands this link with cannibalism as being "exceptional" despite linking it with the colonial discourses of the past which might suggest that race is the consequence of colonial violence. The problem that he sees with these discursive connections is that they create "flat renderings of difference."[79] Ethnography for Dattatreyan provides a corrective to exceed the lack of texture and nuance, the transcultural complexity that constitutes the Somali lived experience in Delhi beyond racism. Such studies like those conducted by Dattatreyan and Singh affirm that the complexity of phenomenological experience and identity bucks the discursive straightjacket of racist logic. In this sense, hip hop studies extend powers reach given its implicit logic which in this instance is nothing more than "a phase in the

[75] Frantz Fanon, *Black Skin, White Masks*, trans. by Charles Lam Markmann (London: Pluto Press, 1986; repr. 2008), 102.

[76] Lindon Barrett, *Racial Blackness and the Discontinuity of Western Modernity* (Champaign: University of Illinois Press, 2013), 1–43.

[77] Fanon, *Black Skin, White Masks*, 95.

[78] Dattatreyan, "Critical hip-hop cinema," 10–11.

[79] Dattatreyan, "Critical hip-hop cinema," 12.

dialectic" of recognition.[80] If they framed the youth in which they worked as social ciphers, rather than overemphasizing identitarian complexity and renegade forms of subjectivity, they would oppose working within a form of political understanding that safeguards the racial schema of the world. In other words, the void of blackness understood as a social cipher, as the outcome of violence, rather than a different cultural constellation, by force majeure personifies refusal; that is "the refusal of any experience that agrees fully with racial common sense, and thus the rejection of any belief that *righting* the "wrong" of blackness could be secured by making blackness a right (to representation) in the present."[81]

This push to elevate the transcultural voice in hip hop studies is an attempt to normalize difference and plurality in community, but at the expense of understanding power. In pushing against, or at least suspending the idea that it is the transcultural that helps develop subversive models for thought and being, blackness no longer becomes part of a project of restoration which does not dispute the abstract universalism of the human and the social.[82] Of course, Somali youth in Delhi, along with other African diasporic populations elsewhere, equally exist in performing complicated forms of subjectivity, but they do not exist in the world equally. Hence the antiblack logic which conditions what they are follows them to India, Italy, Brazil, and beyond. Despite provincializing the human while expanding the social through a mapping of the gradations of lived experience it is the social cipher that poses the inevitable limit to all understanding.

CONCLUSION

In the end, a blackened perspective which centers the social cipher acts as the instrument of possible transcendence, breaking free from the transcultural suture, wallowing freely in dispossession. In other words, agentic language lurks beneath much of what structures hip hop ethnography and therefore, limiting what is beyond the subject. Hip hop ethnography is repetitive, for it is a consequence of only looking and seeking agency, transcultural self-possession at all costs. As hip hop scholars, we have the

---

[80] Fanon, *Black Skin, White Masks,* 111.
[81] David Marriott, *Whither Fanon?: studies in the blackness of being* (Palo Alto: Stanford University Press, 2018) 218. Emphasis in the original.
[82] Mbembe, *Critique of black reason,* 173.

ethical duty to theorize blackness both as a structure and as a fluid identity. Yet, hip hop ethnography reads nothing but identity: a predictable outcome only changed by the subtlety of discourse of which transculturalism is but one example. Hip hop ethnography, whether in India, Italy, or beyond, fails to look beyond its own creations, that is, phenomenological affirmation. Transcultural voices are just another means by which to suture the social cipher to the world, rather than seeing the cipher as refusing to be *of* and *for* the world.

Focusing on the social cipher has ontological implications and vice versa. In other words, narrative construction is a metaphysical activity with limited ontological consequences. The anxiety around emphasizing the incommensurability of the social cipher or as De La Soul once put it, an "anonymous nobody" is replaced by neurotic narratives of social life, a mask that distorts reality bearing aspirational attributes that are neglectful, if not ignorant, of political ontology.[83] Rather than work from the position of the social cipher, hip hop ethnographies are drawn to the transcultural voice for its emotional resonance and ultimate productivity. In repairing a breach in understanding a veil of illusion is spun that treats antiblackness indirectly and with considerable distance. Antiblackness simply becomes the backdrop for agentic accomplishment and in burying the ontological antagonism that is blackness, identity takes political priority. By extension, the racial schema is reconstituted instead of investigating the contradiction of its own identity. In other words, hip hop ethnographies find transcultural nuance at the expense of the Fanonian *tabula rasa*—they neglect to see blackness in the negation of itself, clearing the ground for subjects to grasp their freedom rather than preserve the being that is.[84] Hip hop scholars too often cling to being, rather than abandon it for the void of being, the social cipher.

In the end, hip hop ethnography balks at the meanings and burdens of black identity. What I am proposing is a refusal of narrow categorizations of black identity, transcultural and otherwise, in favor of a notion of blackness as a social cipher. It strikes me that if hip hop is a means of producing social knowledge (known euphemistically as the ledge) about the ways in which humans interact, produce, and make meaning in the world around

---

[83] De La Soul, *And the Anonymous Nobody*, 2016, Kobalt.

[84] See, Frantz Fanon, *The Wretched of the Earth*, trans. by C. Farrington. London: Penguin, 1961[1990]. For a deep and extended reading of Fanon's tabula rasa see Marriott, *Whither Fanon*.

them, then it stands that what it means to be human within the social must be fundamental to any ethnographic approach. As Ramírez-D'Oleo, Dixa has stated, "Scholarship whose function is to analyze, critique, de-sediment, and question without necessarily being equally concerned with the work of *creating*—beyond the critique itself—remains crucial in a world barreling into increasingly obvious fascisms."[85] To this end, the descriptive argument here is not that experiential accounts of transcultural blackness and hip hop are incorrect, but flagrantly incomplete. Bypassing the social cipher is a principle of modernity itself—regression into an anti-black world. If hip hop studies was ethically and authentically committed to freeing blackness from its wretchedness, from social death, it would not take flight in transcultural dreamscapes, but embrace the radical abyss of freedom qua contradiction. In ethically "doing the knowledge," hip hop ethnography would understand that the social cipher is the counterforce and counter memory that ruptures what it means to be. So, when the knowledge of the social cipher finally displaces, eliminates, and replaces the academic hegemony of the transcultural cipher, so be it!

BIBLIOGRAPHY

Alim, H. Samy. *Roc the mic right: The language of hip hop culture.* New York: Routledge, 2006.

Alim, H. Sammy, and Alistair Pennycook. *Global linguistic flows.* New York: Taylor & Francis, 2008.

Appadurai, Arjun. *Modernity at large: Cultural dimensions of globalization.* Minneapolis: U of Minnesota Press, 1996.

Barrett, Lindon. *Racial Blackness and the Discontinuity of Western Modernity.* Champaign: University of Illinois Press, 2013.

Bernard, Patrick S. "A "Cipher Language"." *African American Review* 52.2 (2019): 121-142.

Bey, Marquis. *The Problem of the Negro as a Problem for Gender.* Minneapolis: University of Minnesota Press, 2020.

Brand Nubian. *In God We Trust.* 1993. Elektra Records.

Cambridge Dictionary, Accessed June 2, 2024 https://dictionary.cambridge. org/us/dictionary/english/cipher

Chang, Jeff, ed. *Total chaos: The art and aesthetics of hip-hop.* New York: Civitas Books, 2006.

---

[85] Dixa Ramírez-D'Oleo, *This Will Not Be Generative* (Cambridge: Cambridge University Press, 2023), 4–5.

Chipato, Farai, and David Chandler. "The black horizon: Alterity and ontology in the Anthropocene." *Global Society* 37, no. 2 (2023): 157-175.

Crawford, Margo Natalie. *Black Post-Blackness: The Black Arts Movement and Twenty-First-Century Aesthetics.* Champaign: University of Illinois Press, 2017.

Culp, Andrew. *Dark Deleuze.* Minneapolis: University of Minnesota Press, 2016.

Dattatreyan, Gabriel. "Critical hip-hop cinema: Racial logics and ethnographic ciphas in Delhi." *Wide Screen* 7, no. 1 (2018): 1-27.

Dattatreyan, Ethiraj Gabriel. *The Globally Familiar: Digital Hip Hop, Masculinity, and Urban Space in Delhi.* Durham: Duke University Press, 2020.

De La Soul. *And the Anonymous Nobody.* 2016. Kobalt.

Dimitriadis, Greg. "Framing hip hop: New methodologies for new times." *Urban Education* 50.1 (2015): 31-51.

Dolasinski, Lisa. "'In Between' Ethnic Heritage and Italian Identity: The Global Hip-Hop of Mahmood and Ghali." *The Italianist* 42, no. 1 (2022): 119-138.

DuBois, *Dusk of Dawn: The Autobiography of W.E.B. DuBois.* New York: Harcourt 1940.

Earthgang. *Rags.* 2017. Interscope.

Fanon, Frantz. *The Wretched of the Earth*, trans. by C. Farrington. London: Penguin, 1961[1990].

———. *Black Skin, White Masks*, trans. by C. Markmann. London: Pluto Press, 1986 [2008].

Fernandes, Sujatha. *Close to the edge: In search of the global hip hop generation.* New York: Verso Books, 2011.

Gibson, J. J. "The theory of affordances." In R. Shaw & J. Bransford, eds., *Perceiving, acting, and knowing.* 67–82. Hillsdale: Lawrence Erlbaum, 1977.

Harrison, Kwame Anthony. "Hip-hop and racial identification: an (auto)ethnographic perspective." In Justin A. Williams, ed. *The Cambridge Companion to Hip-Hop.* 152-167. Cambridge: Cambridge University Press; 2015.

Hart, William David. *The Blackness of Black: Key Concepts in Critical Discourse.* Lanham, MD: Rowman & Littlefield, 2020.

Hawthorne, Camilla. *Contesting race and citizenship: youth politics in the Black Mediterranean.* Ithaca: Cornell University Press, 2022.

Henson, Bryce. *Emergent Quilombos: Black Life and Hip-Hop in Brazil.* Austin: University of Texas Press, 2023,

Holt, Kevin C. "Emcee Ethnographies: A Brief Sketch of US Hip-Hop Ethnography." (2019): 6-20.

Ibrahim, Awad. "Arab Spring, favelas, borders, and the artistic transnational migration: Toward a curriculum for a global hip-hop nation." In Toukan, Elena V., Rubèn A. Gaztambide-Fernandez, and Sardar M. Anwaruddin, eds. *Curriculum of Global Migration and Transnationalism.* 103-111. New York: Routledge, 2020.

Jay Z. *4:44,* 2017. Roc Nation.

Jeffries, Michael P. "Hip-hop Urbanism Old and New." *International Journal of Urban and Regional Research* 38, no. 2 (2014): 706-715.

Judy, Ronald A. *Sentient flesh: Thinking in disorder, poiēsis in black*. Durham: Duke University Press, 2020.

Jung, Moon-Kie, and João H. Costa Vargas. "More than and beyond racism: theoretical and political meditations on antiblackness." *Souls* 23.3-4 (2022): n.p.

Karera, Axelle. "Paraontology: interruption, inheritance, or a debt one often regrets." *Critical Philosophy of Race* 10, no. 2 (2022): 158-197.

Marriott, David. *Whither Fanon?: studies in the blackness of being*. Palo Alto: Stanford University Press, 2018.

———. "On Crystallization." *Critical Times* 4, no. 2 (2021): 187-232.

Mbembe, Achille. *Critique of black reason*. Durham: Duke University Press, 2017.

Morgado, Marcos. "Translocal Hip Hop Aesthetics: Contemporary Performances in Brazilian Hip Hop." In Williams, Quentin, and Jaspal Naveel Singh, eds. *Global hiphopography*. 273-298 London: Palgrave Macmillan, 2023.

Morgan, Marcyliena. *Hip-Hop en Français: An Exploration of Hip-Hop Culture in the Francophone World*. Rowman & Littlefield, 2020.

Moten, Fred. "The case of blackness." *Criticism* 50.2 (2008): 177-218.

Osumare, Halifu. "Keeping it Real: Race, Class, and Youth Connections Through Hip-Hop in the US & Brazil." *Humboldt Journal of Social Relations* 37 (2015): 6-18.

———. *The Africanist aesthetic in global hip-hop: Power moves*. Cham: Springer, 2016.

Pennycook, Alastair. *Global Englishes and Transcultural Flows*. New York: Routledge, 2006.

Perry, Imani. *Prophets of the hood: Politics and poetics in hip hop*. Durham: Duke University Press, 2004.

Peterson, James Braxton. "A Cipher of the Underground in Black Literary Culture." In *The Hip-Hop Underground and African American Culture: Beneath the Surface*. 83-99. New York: Palgrave Macmillan, 2014.

Poor Righteous Teachers. *Pure Poverty*. 1991. Profile Records.

Ramírez-D'Oleo, Dixa. *This Will Not Be Generative*. Cambridge: Cambridge University Press, 2023

Rose, Tricia. *Black noise: Rap music and Black cultural resistance in contemporary American popular culture*. Middletown: Wesleyan University, 1994.

Saucier, P. Khalil, ed. *Native Tongues: An African Hip Hop Reader*. Trenton: Africa World Press, 2011.

———. "Continental drift: the politics and poetics of African hip hop." In *Sounds and the City: Popular Music, Place, and Globalization*, pp. 196-208. London: Palgrave Macmillan UK, 2014.

Saucier, P. Khalil, and Kumarini Silva. "Keeping it real in the global south: Hip-hop comes to Sri Lanka." *Critical Sociology* 40, no. 2 (2014): 295-300.

Scarparo, Susanna, and Mathias Sutherland Stevenson. *Reggae and hip hop in southern Italy: Politics, languages, and multiple marginalities.* Cham, Switzerland: Springer, 2018.

Scarparo, Susanna, and Mathias Sutherland Stevenson. "Transcultural flows and marginality: reggae and hip hop in Sardinia." *Modern Italy* 25, no. 2 (2020): 199-212.

Sexton, Jared. "Affirmation in the Dark." *The Comparatist* 43 (2019): 90-111.

Singh, Jaspal Naveel. *Transcultural voices: Narrating hip hop culture in complex Delhi.* Bristol: Multilingual Matters, 2021.

Sithole, Tendayi. *The Black Register.* New York: Polity, 2020.

Spady, James G. "Mapping and Re-Membering Hip Hop History, Hiphopography and African Diasporic History." *Western Journal of Black Studies* 37, no. 2 (2013): 126-157.

Spady, James G., Samir Meghelli, and H. Samy Alim. *Tha Global Cipha: Hip hop Culture and Consciousness.* Philadelphia: Black History Museum Press, 2006.

Spillers, Hortense J. *Black, white, and in color: Essays on American literature and culture.* Chicago: University of Chicago Press, 2003.

Spivak, Gayatri Chakravorty. "Can the subaltern speak?." In Cain, Peter J., and Mark Harrison, eds. *Imperialism: critical concepts in historical studies.* Vol. 3. 171-219. New York: Taylor & Francis, 2004.

Thomas, Greg. "Wynter with Fanon in the FLN: The "Rights of Peoples" against the "Monohumanism" of "Man"." *American Quarterly* 70.4 (2018): 857-865.

Vernon, Jim. *Sampling, biting, and the postmodern subversion of hip hop.* Cham, Switzerland; Palgrave Macmillan, 2021.

Williams, Quentin, and Jaspal Naveel Singh. "Introduction: Hip Hop's Here, There… and Everywhere—An Introduction to Global Hiphopography." In Williams, Quentin, and Jaspal Naveel Singh, eds. *Global hiphopography.* 1-25. London: Palgrave Macmillan, 2023.

Wynter, Sylvia. "Unsettling the coloniality of being/power/truth/freedom: Towards the human, after man, its overrepresentation—An argument." *CR: The new centennial review* 3, no. 3 (2003): 257-337.

Wynter, S., and K. McKittrick. "Unparalleled catastrophe for our species? Or, to give humanness a different future: Conversations." In K. McKittrick, ed. *Sylvia Wynter: On being human as praxis.* 9–89. Durham: Duke University Press, 2015.

Zalloua, Zahi. *Being Posthuman: Ontologies of the Future.* London: Bloomsbury, 2021.

Jay-Z's ~~Afropessimism~~ Black Femme(inism)s Makes ~~Black~~ All Life Matter

M. Shadee Malaklou

> If black women were free, it would mean that everyone else would have to be free since [black women's] freedom would necessitate the destruction of all the systems of oppression.[1]

> It should be clear to those who read this literature that Afro-pessimism is made possible by the critical labors of a particular strand of *Black* feminisms, a la [Saidiya] Hartman and [Hortense] Spillers.[2]

---

[1] Combahee River Collective, "A Black Feminist Statement," *Home Girls, A Black Feminist Anthology*, ed. Barbara Smith (New York: Kitchen Table: Women of Color Press, Inc., 1983).
[2] Frank B. Wilderson III and Shannon Walsh, "Afro-pessimism and Friendship in South Africa: An Interview with Frank B. Wilderson III," in *Ties that Bind: Race and the Politics of Friendship in South Africa,* ed. Shannon Walsh and John Soske (Johannesburg: Wits University Press, 2016).

M. S. Malaklou (✉)
Berea College, Department of Women's, Gender, and Sexuality Studies, Berea, KY, USA
e-mail: mlakloum@berea.edu

To engage the black femme(inism)s[3] that underwrite afropessimism's paradigmatic critique—its critique of structure, or form—I asked my students in "Black Lives (Don't) Matter," an upper-division theory course, and in "Gender, Sexuality, and Black Lives Matter," an introductory special topics course, to listen to and watch Jay-Z's visual album *4:44*.[4]

Doing so prompted a critique of liberal humanism that was also a critical opening. In navigating the chaos and cacophony of *4:44*—not (just) with their minds, but sensorially—students mined the antiblack violence afropessimism describes as social death for black femme(inist) lessons on survivance. They read for movement and meaning not as linear progression, but in the music video's fits and starts, refusing easy understandings of social death, in flattened terms, as a closed door to relationality. Students instead learned from the black femme(inist)s who built afropessimism's house of resistance—and remain there still, as its custodians[5]—to imagine Other socialities, unknown and unbossed and unbought, in the "elsewhere and elsewhen" that social death's portal (i.e., liberal humanism's closure) opens.[6] Like Jay-Z, whose success is subtended by Beyoncè's genius, afropessimism is made viable (i.e., made alive), Frank B. Wilderson III reflects in the epigraph, through the "critical labors" of black femme(inist)s.[7] Wilderson names only two contemporary scholars—Hortense Spillers and Saidiya Hartman, both of whom appear in the music video for "4:44"—obscuring important contributions also from black femme(inist) elders and ancestors, "m/others" and aunties who staged afropessimism's critique before afropessimism arrived with a name.[8] We do

---

[3] This Otherwise is a feminine and feminized articulation of space and especially, of time. I therefore use the term "femme(inism)s" for two reasons. The first reason is to distinguish black women's gender struggle—constant and unyielding—from the ebb and flow of "her"-story. And second, to underscore the racialized woman's work that births afropessimism *and* subtends all that we know under the signpost of the human, or being.

[4] Jay Z. *4:44*, 2017. Roc Nation.

[5] Angela Davis, "Reflections on the Black Woman's Role in the Community of Slaves," *The Massachusetts Review* 13, no. 1/2 (Winter - Spring 1972, "Woman: An Issue").

[6] Fred Moten, "Blackness and Nothingness (Mysticism in the Flesh)," *South Atlantic Quarterly*
12, no. 4 (2013): 746.

[7] Wilderson III, "Afro-pessimism and Friendship in South Africa."

[8] Alexis Pauline Gumbs, "m/other ourselves: a Black queer femme(inist) genealogy for radical mothering," *Revolutionary Mothering: Love on the Front Lines*, ed. Alexis Pauline Gumbs, China Martens and Mai'a Williams (PM Press 2016). This is Alexis Pauline Gumbs'

not just owe the teeth of our critique to these black femme(inist)s. We owe our lives—*all life*—to them. One cannot deny that many of afropessimism's most novel and scandalous claims have already been said *with consequence* by black women; for example, by bell hooks, who, until the day she died, was heartbroken that the world so discredited and humiliated her when she dared to suggest, in conversation with Janel Mock in 2014, that Beyoncè may very well be "colluding in the construction of herself as a slave."[9] Four years later, the *New York Times* would publish an interview with Wilderson about his monograph *Afropessimism*, taking seriously the same question: *what does it mean to be a slave?*[10]

Jay-Z is a problematic bedfellow for black femme(inism)s for the same reasons that he is an easy friend to afropessimism. While his company Roc Nation's[11] problematic partnership with the NFL, and his commercialism and masculinism more generally, betray his shortcomings, Jay-Z's attention to the criminal injustice system, his personal contributions to disaster relief (for example, in Puerto Rico)[12] and to protestors' bail in Ferguson and Baltimore, as well as his fundraising efforts for the families of Sean Bell and Trayvon Martin, and more recently, the $20 million dollars Jay-Z raised to send financially distressed persons to college, to list just a few examples, are—as exercises of black futurity—undoubtedly black femme(inist) commitments.[13]

Collaborating with acclaimed artist and filmmaker Arthur Jafa, a long-time conversation partner to the named and unnamed black femme(inist) s in afropessimism's project, to produce the music video for "4:44,"

"name for that nurturing work, that survival dance, worked by enslaved women who were forced to breastfeed the children of the status mothers while having no control over whether their birth or chosen children were sold away." In this way, m/Othering is "less [...] a gendered identity and more a possible action, a technology of transformation" that teaches us to live Otherwise (Gumbs 2016, 22–23).

[9] Mikki Kendall, "bell hooks pushed us to think harder about feminism, Black women and Beyonce," *The Washington Post*, December 16, 2021. n.p.

[10] John Williams, "In 'Afropessimism,' a Black Intellectual Mixes Memoir and Theory," *The New York Times*, April 5, 2020; Frank B. Wilderson III, *Afropessimism* (New York: Liveright, 2020).

[11] Jay-Z founded the entertainment company Roc Nation in 2008.

[12] Sarah Jasmine Montgomery, "Jay-Z's 40/40 Club is hosting a fundraiser to help Puerto Rico," *Fader*, October 4, 2017.

[13] Ashley Iasimone, "Jay-Z's Shawn Carter Foundation Raises $20 Million at 20th Anniversary Gala in New York," *Billboard*, July 15, 2023.

Jay-Z's aesthetic choices further query form, posing afropessimism's metaphysical critique as a black femme(inist) problem *and possibility*. If racial blackness is Man's constant and unmoving (and un/gendered) Other, defined by stasis (i.e., social death) so that Man can define himself as he who moves; then racial blackness—as the "zero degree" of Man's "social conceptualization"—is the constitutive outside that makes possible all we know and name as *form*, or being, to exist in the first place.[14]

Visual media offers context or *mise-en-scene*, presumably distant and apart from our own worlding, that is a self-contained form or structure for conversations about how a medium's container—or metaphysics, or space-time—*produces* subjectivity, or objecthood (i.e., racial blackness), as it were. When paired with Beyoncè's *Lemonade*,[15] *4:44* betrays the "racial calculus" and/as "political arithmetic" whereby liberal humanism invites some persons of color to sit at its table of meaning-making, animating Man's political-economic structures and social and psychic worlds[16]; while others—namely, racially black people—arrive to the table of human civilization, as Frantz Fanon argues in *Black Skin, White Masks*, "too soon"[17]— at the dawn of Man, where "x" marks the spot of Man's "zero degree"—*and* "too late," which is to say, not at all.[18]

As *Lemonade*'s beneficiary, *4:44* inherits the feminine and feminized articulation of space and especially, of time, that Beyoncè and her black femme(inist) kinfolk twerk and werk without the promise of arrival or the ruse of phallic mastery. The many empty buses, parking lots, and other failed means of transportation in *Lemonade* go nowhere and "lead *everywhere*," carrying us by portal and time machine, goading us to "leap" into the living conjured by and prepared for us by the black women and femmes who refuse to be had.[19]

---

[14] Hortense Spillers, "Mama's Baby, Papa's Maybe: An American Grammar Book," *Diacritics* 17, no. 2 (1987): 67.

[15] Beyonce. *Lemonade*. 2016. Parkwood Entertainment.

[16] Saidiya Hartman, *Lose Your Mother: A Journey Along the Atlantic Slave Route* (Farrar, Straus and Giroux 2007), 6.

[17] Frantz Fanon, *Black Skin, White Masks*, trans. Charles Lam Markmann (London: Pluto Press, 1986).

[18] Spillers, "Mama's Baby, Papa's Maybe," 67.

[19] Jared Sexton, "The Social Life of Social Death: On Afro-Pessimism and Black Optimism," *InTensions* 5 (Fall/Winter 2011): 9; Fanon, *Black Skin, White Masks*, 229.

MAKING ~~BLACK~~ *ALL* LIFE MATTER

It was before the emergence of Donald Trump's white supremacist America, in the hour of the first multi-racial president, that we learned an important lesson: black lives do not matter. Barack Obama's presidency—won not because he is half black, but because he is half white, embodying the triumph of white forms of being and doing and knowing over racially black ones—demonstrated that black lives will be sacrificed to the alter of white supremacy irrespective of a new "post"-racial or "colorblind"—in other words, liberal—America. Those of us who have been paying attention to the vernacular interventions of black women and femmes know that this is not a new lesson, even as afropessimism would have us believe that its critique singularly arrived to make such claims over and against the "diversity and inclusion" efforts that characterize our post-civil rights moment.

Even Jay-Z has been telling us that black life does not (cannot) matter in a multi-racial world; and that a project committed to making black (women's) lives matter first/last/only will make *all life matter.* Jay-Z's politics, at least as he elaborates them in the lyrics to "Legacy," wants our political awakening. He asks those among us with means to "take those moneys and spread [them] 'cross families',," to create a "society within a society" in which we take care of each other. With *4:44,* Jay-Z models what Denise Ferreira da Silva describes as a black femme(inist) *poethics* of care, understanding that the marital redemption he seeks will require him to enact love as the political demand for social justice.[20]

UPSETTING VISUAL MEDIA'S LIBIDINAL ANTIBLACKNESS

To teach *4:44* as a black femme(inist) lesson requires thinking with visual media to access and disarticulate the *libidinal economy* of—the unconscious drives and "structures of feeling" attendant to—antiblackness.[21] Absent this co-curricular investment, a class with the mandate to teach "Black Lives Matter" would reify black matter/ing as a liberal humanist project. Such containment practices, which are germane even/especially

---

[20] See Denise Ferreira da Silva, "Toward a Black Femme(inist) Poethics: The Quest(ion) of Blackness Toward the End of the World," *The Black Scholar* 44, no. 2 (2014): 81–97; bell hooks, *All About Love: New Visions* (New York: William Morrow Paperback, 2018).

[21] See Raymond Williams and Michael Orrom, *Preface to Film* (London: Film Drama Limited, 1954).

to black studies programs and departments, think racial blackness as a human identity or category of difference, rather than as that assemblage of being and doing and knowing which upsets the entire enterprise of the human, and thus, which serves as a generative terrain for metaphysical questions—what Jared Sexton describes as "the posing of [the] question [of being], rather than imitation of a form of being"—in a wide range of classrooms, including Black Studies, Ethnic Studies, Whiteness Studies, Critical Identity Studies, Women's and Gender (and Sexuality) Studies, and beyond.[22]

Wilderson and Sexton have argued that in addition to animating the political-economic structures that make black flesh and black forms of social life accumulable and fungible, the onto-epistemic break brokered by Enlightenment humanism and its attendant technologies, like the transatlantic and Indian Ocean slave trades, induced a *libidinal economy* that has since overdetermined our structures of feeling, turning our "viscera, guts, and instincts"—that is, our psychic-unconscious processes—against racial blackness.[23]

Afropessimists borrow and rehabilitate the term *libidinal economy* from Jean-Francois Lyotard, who first used the concept in 1974 to think about the "intensities" of the libido as they contribute to a metaphysics of desire.[24] But, for afropessimists—and for the black femme(inist)s who came before and whose work propels afropessimism's critique (e.g., Hortense Spillers, whose opens "Mama's Baby, Papa's Maybe" with anatomical descriptions of rupture like those in Lyotard's first chapter)— this libidinal economy is at once individual *and* collective. Individual psychic protocols of recognition and perception are, as Sylvia Wynter elaborates, "*semantically-neurochemically*" induced to feed "the performative enactment of our ensemble of always already role-allocated [i.e., antiblack] individual and collective behaviors."[25] The individual psyche is overdetermined from without, which is to say: is overdetermined by a grammar that inscribes an antiblack logos, pathos, and ethos to human

[22] Sexton, "The Social Life of Social Death," 9.
[23] See M. Shadee Malaklou, "'Teaching Trayvon' at Irvine: On Femme(inist) Praxis, Afropessimism, and 'Woke Work,'" *National Political Science Review* 18 (December 2016), n.p.
[24] Jean-Francois Lyotard, *Libidinal Economy*, trans. Iain Hamilton Grant (Bloomington: Indiana University Press, 1993).
[25] Sylvia Wynter, "Unparalleled catastrophe for our species?," in *Sylvia Wynter: On Being Human as Praxis*, ed. Katherine McKittrick (Durham: Duke University Press, 2015), 32–33. Emphasis in the original.

material operations and semantic-neurochemical contemplations. Stated another way, individual psychic protocols are informed by a collective unconscious that is governed by antiblack "energies, concerns, points of attention, anxieties, pleasures, appetites, revulsions, and phobias," such that we are "law-likely" to consume black culture and sociality, but to discard with black people.[26]

Notably, black femme(inist)s staged a potent critique of this libidinal economy long before afropessimism emerged within the academy as a kind of black study. In 1980, Audre Lorde taught us about the psychic-unconscious structures of antiblackness when she famously wrote that the master's tools would not dismantle the master's house; more specifically, when she wrote that "we have, built into all of us, old blueprints of expectation and response," and that "these must be altered at the same time as we alter the living conditions which are a result of those structures."[27] Lorde's treatise is primarily concerned with a praxis that will save *the earth* rather than the (human) world, including how we might imagine that world otherwise, which Sexton describes as our (bad) faith in "the whole possibility of and desire for a world."[28] Indeed, it is a black femme(inist) lesson—and not necessarily, primarily, or exclusively afropessimism's lesson—that black people have been made coeval with earth-matter (at best, with a sentient matter that *does not matter*, and at worst, with non-sentient object-things) and that we must reimagine our relationship to the earth if we are to make black life matter *structurally.*

Perhaps counterintuitively, I do not sidestep this libidinal economy in my approach to black study. Instead, I ask students to interrogate the operations of the unconscious as they are sociogenically engineered by visual media, as a way to engage in a discussion of the unthought, in other words, in order to walk a forbidden terrain, locating coherence not at the level of narrative but at a different scale and scope—one of ethics. Which is to say, I assign media texts to my students precisely *because* these representations appeal to the unconscious; because rather than absolve us of the antiblack racism that justifies antiblack violence, these representations are the preferred medium for the communicability of—as Wilderson argues in

---

[26] Frank B. Wilderson III, *Red, White & Black: Cinema and the Structure of U.S. Antagonisms* (Durham: Duke University Press, 2010), 7; Wynter, "Unparalleled catastrophe for our species?"

[27] Audre Lorde, "Age, Race, Class, and Sex: Women Redefining Difference," in *Sister Outsider: Essays and Speeches by Audre Lorde* (Berkeley: Crossing Press 2007), 123.

[28] Sexton, "The Social Life of Social Death," 31.

his defense of afropessimism—the ideologies that are attendant to our gross accumulation of black flesh and to black death.[29]

While it is true that an antiblack libidinal economy is epistemic, and while I am arguing that an afropessimistic classroom that is also, or primarily, a black femme(inist) classroom engages the regimes of *over-*representations that impress this economy, my approach takes care to use these images to goad students into disarticulating their faith in the unconscious as a site of ethicality; in other words, to dislodge their faith that that deep down, inside, in the heart and in the constitution of one's conscience, there is some right and good truth about how to inhabit this world that would amount to an ethical orientation. To the extent that an afropessimist *qua* black femme(inist) engagement with visual media upsets this expectation, it asks students to locate structure as that which is *within the self* at the same time as it is, primarily, *outside the self.* Students are thus instructed to read/watch/listen for what *punches them in the gut*, to be on the lookout for what either appeals to their viscera, guts, and/or instincts or disarticulates those processes. They consider how their deepest energies and compulsions are governed from without, impressed by a visual media regime that (at least in the United States) had its start in antiblack imagery, specifically, in Jim Crow imagery.

In *4:44,* Jay-Z upsets this libidinal economy by ingeniously using antiblack tropes to disabuse us of visual media's pedagogy. He leans into the social death that these images exemplify *because he knows* there is no social life without social death. He especially does this when he recounts the caricatures circumscribing his (non)being in "The Story of O.J." As the first single to materialize from *4:44,* "The Story of O.J." samples Nina Simone's "Four Women"[30] to make an argument that black lives, irrespective of any particular black person's bid for wealth or status (i.e., regardless of one's hue: "light n***a, dark n***a," or stature: "rich n***a, poor n***a, house n***a, field n***a"), are still definitively "n***a"—in other words, they still don't (or perhaps, can't) matter in humanist terms.

What Jay-Z imparts is the lesson that our viscera, guts, and instincts are committed to consuming these images of the Other—are committed to "eating" the Other, as bell hooks wrote long before afropessimists ever engaged Lyotard's idea of a *libidinal economy.*[31] The haunting sample of

[29] See Wilderson III, *Red, White & Black.*
[30] Nina Simone. *Wild as the Wind.* 1966. Philips.
[31] Lyotard, *Libidinal Economy.*

Simone's "Four Women" in "The Story of O.J." only further suggests that black women carry this burden for the rest of us, as a racial-sexual terror. In other words, it is the backdrop of Simone's intervention that reminds listeners that patriarchy and misogyny—that the sexism that names (and cannot differentiate between) Simone as "Aunt Sarah" and "Saffronia" and "Sweet thing" and "Peaches"—are symptoms or technologies of the same antiblack violence that makes black life accumulable and fungible. "The Story of O.J." thus imparts the important lesson that black women do the work—the quiet and unrecognized domestic and background labor—to make black life matter even/especially when they don't, for example, even/especially when black people are caricatured as "happy darkies" (i.e., "dark n***a") or as buffoons and dandies (i.e., "rich n***a").

If mass visual media in the United States *began* with the circulation of antiblack tropes, then these tropes—emerging at the hour of abolition—have a pedagogical function: to teach Americans that chattel slavery is a social good and that the emancipation of slaves would unleash black peoples' criminal and sexual passions. In "The Story of O.J.," Jay-Z encourages black people to abandon the lie that tells them that if they put on the human trappings that serve to (at least cosmetically) distance their bodies and (as) their selves from these caricatures of racial blackness, as O.J. attempted to do as a "rich n***a," then they will not be shot dead in the streets or lynched in the courtroom. Which is to say, Jay-Z's is the black femme(inist) lesson that Jamilah Lemieux imparted at the height of the Black Lives Matter movement: that black people should "stop trying to be good," which has never been about racial blackness, and instead should try harder to "be black"—that is, because they're going to try to kill you anyways.[32]

UPSETTING VISUAL MEDIA'S HUMANIST PEDAGOGY

A visual media approach to black study serves to illustrate that antiblack violence is not just inherent to humanism as a libidinal-economic project, but that it is also inherent to media as a humanist pedagogy; indeed, that media is the preferred mode of communicability for humanism's libidinal-economic project. In the end, this libidinal-economic project is committed to justifying the killing black people any which way, regardless of

---

[32] Jamilah Lemieux, "Stop Trying to Be Good—Be Black." *Mic* (June 30, 2015).

whether or how the black person in question performs the humanist mim-
icry that might allow them to temporarily evade the caricatures that pre-
scribe their death, as O.J. models.

A visual media approach to black study requires that we re/think our
ways of feeling and looking (i.e., the gaze)[33] at the same time as we re/
imagine our relationship to the earth (as opposed to the world), if we are
to make black life matter against humanist odds. It must additionally take
care to avoid spectacles of the Other and "scenes of subjection" that leave
students chomping at the bit for more of the same.[34] Given this constraint,
the genius of popular culture artists like Jay-Z and Beyoncè are all the
more significant. Such new forms of radical black experimentation outside
of academia inherit the rich, long history of the black avant garde, which
is evidence enough that afropessimism's black femme(inist) critique has
been around long before afropessimism's name, and that this black
femme(inist) critique originates from the same "streets" that make black
lives accumulable and fungible.

Insofar as black grammars of suffering and the *anagrammaticality*[35] of
black living or sociality are questions not for/from liberal humanist
academia, but "the streets"—where black people do not have a right to
stand on the sidewalk (as Trayvon Martin's murder taught us) or even, to

---

[33] bell hooks begins to theorize such im/possibilities in her conceptualization of an "oppo-
sitional gaze." See *Black Looks: Race and Representation* (Boston: South End Press, 1992).

[34] Saidiya Hartman, *Scenes of Subjection: Terror, Slavery, and Self-Making in Nineteenth-
Century America* (New York: Oxford University Press, 1997).

[35] This is Christina Sharpe's term, see *In the Wake: On Blackness and Being* (Durham: Duke
University Press, 2016). Sharpe explains that racial blackness is *anagrammatical* insofar as
"we can see the moments when blackness opens up … in the literal sense as when 'a word,
phrase, or name is formed by rearranging the letters of another' (*Merriam-Webster Online*).
We can also apprehend this in the metaphorical sense in how, regarding blackness, grammatical gender galls away and new meanings proliferate; how 'the letters of a text are formed into
a secret message by rearranging them' or a secret message is discovered through the rearranging of the letters of a text. *Ana-*, as a prefix, means 'up, in place of time, back, again,
anew.' So, blackness anew, blackness as a/temporal, in and out of place and time putting
pressure on meaning and that against which meaning is made. We see this again and again
how, in and out of the United States … *girl* doesn't mean 'girl' but, for example, 'prostitute'
or 'felon,' *boy* doesn't mean 'boy,' but 'Hulk Hogan' or 'gunman,' 'thug' or 'urban youth.'
We see that *mother* doesn't mean 'mother,' but 'felon' and 'defender' and/or 'birther of terror' and not one of the principal grounds of terrors [sic] multiple and quotidian enact-
ments. … As the meaning of words fall apart, we encounter again and again the difficult of
sticking the signification. This is Black being in the wake. This is the anagrammatical. These
are Black lives, annotated" (Sharpe 2016, 76–77).

breathe (as Eric Garner's murder suggests)—afropessimism's black femme(inist) critique is especially salient for querying popular culture. Since what is at stake in—not black *studies*, which codifies and commodifies black social life, but—black *study* is antiblack violence producing not subjective coherence or institutional legibility but objective and narrative incoherence, afropessimism's black femme(inist) methodological insights call for the deployment of multiple modes of writing and reading, including those that engage visual media. The goal of afropessimism—and, if we pay attention to afropessimism's citational practices, the goal of the black femme(inism)s that animates its critique—is to stay with what Dionne Brand describes the "tear" in the world that is inaugurated by chattel slavery and its "afterlives," and to inhabit the critical' materialisms that this tear generates.[36]

To be sure, ~~an afropessimistic~~ black femme(inist) approach to black study that stays with this "tear" cannot endeavor the masculinist project of reconstituting a whole. Instead, it must do the black femme(inist) work of leaning into racial blackness as a materialism[37] that destabilizes the concept and promise of wholeness.[38] That is to say, a black femme(inist) approach

---

[36] See Brand, *A Map to the Door of No Return*; Hartman, *Scenes of Subjection*.

[37] Racial blackness is primarily raw material for human world-making. The slave, for example, was (is) consumed/consumable for its parts, including skin, hair, bones, organs, and (the story of Henrietta Lacks teaches us) cells. Such practices, like the amassing of lynching souvenirs—well-documented by Ida B. Wells and others—reduce black people to bits and pieces of flesh for human consumption. Hortense Spillers in "Mama's Baby, Papa's Maybe" makes a similar observation about the always already atomized black body rendered flesh for consumption, writing that this body is typified by "eyes beaten out, arms, backs, skills branded, a left jaw, a right ankle, punctured; teeth missing, as the calculated work of iron, whips, chains, knives ... the bullet." Spillers elaborates, "The procedures adopted for the captive flesh demarcate a total objectification, as the entire captive community becomes a living laboratory" (1987, 67, 68).

[38] From a psychoanalytic perspective, it is the black person's gratuitous vulnerability—in other words: ultimate *penetrability*—which characterizes racial blackness as the human's hyper-feminized Other. As Lewis Gordon argues in *Bad Faith and Antiblack Racism* (Humanities Press International, 1995), even black men (and, we might add: gender nonconforming persons) are always already feminized as—in Hortense Spillers' formulation—"female flesh ungendered," and therefore, as the "zero degree" of "social conceptualization" (1987, 67), insofar as they exist outside of the symbolic order that recognizes gender difference.

Gordon explains the inevitable feminization of racial blackness by way of juxtaposing the masculinity of racial whiteness to the feminization of black masculinity. He writes, "Consider the white man. Being pure Presence, he is equated with manliness in toto. The manly, or masculine, is in fact a figure of denial, a being who attempts to close all its holes and become

works to unhinge students' faith in "the world"—and, as Wynter wants us to think about: the *word*.[39] It also, following Sexton, disrupts "maybe even the whole possibility of and desire for a world" or word that might arrive at wholeness or which might suggest that racial blackness can arrive at a stable category of difference that might render it an intra-human conflict.[40] To describe racial blackness in this way—as an identity—is not only disingenuous, but such descriptions also serve to evacuate racial blackness of its radical potentiality to teach us another an/Other way to live.

A black study that impresses the im/possibilities for this Other social living throws the onto-epistemic order of the human—at the level of form, narrative, the dialectic, and all those other symptoms that (white) critical theory teaches in its study of structure to evade the ethical question of the human's essential antiblackness—into crisis, teaching students to question, indeed, to always and restlessly be suspicious of Man and his/her/their-story. Such an approach further encourages students to imagine what might exist outside of the human frame, in the "elsewhere and elsewhen" at the end of our world.[41] But, if—as Sun Ra's Afro-futurism and critical black fabulations like Alexis Pauline Gumbs' *M Archive: After the End of the World* suggest—the present already exists "after" the end of the black world, then black people and especially black artists like Jay-Z and Beyoncè

---

pure, sealed flesh [a 'whole'] in search of holes. From the perspective of such a being, all holes are elsewhere; he doesn't even have an anus; when he kisses, nothing enters his mouth—he enters the Other's. In his presence, the black becomes a chasm to fill. But the black 'man' is a *hole*. ... [The penis] protrudes. It pretends not to be a hole, but instead, a filler-of-holes. ... As pure Presence, masculinity is an ideal form of whiteness with its own gradations; the less of a hole one 'is,' the more masculine one is; the less dark, the more white. The black man would therefore have the propensity to become slimy if it were not for the fact that he embodies femininity even more than the white woman. His skin, his eyes, his nose, his ears, his mouth, his anus, his penis ooze out his femininity like blood from a splattered body. He faces the possibility of denying his feminine situation: a black man in the presence of whiteness stands as a hole to be filled; he stands to the white man in a homoerotic situation and to the white woman in a heterosexual erotic situation with a homoerotic twist; she becomes the white/male that fills his blackness/femininity. ... The black man is caught. He cannot reject his femininity without simultaneously rejecting his blackness, for his femininity stands as a consequence of his blackness and vice versa. Standing in front of a white [human] wall, he appears as a hole, as a gaping, feminine symbol to be filled, closed up, by the being who has being" (Gordon 1995, 127–128, original emphasis).

[39] See Wynter, "Unparalleled catastrophe for our species?"

[40] Sexton, "The Social Life of Social Death," 31.

[41] Fred Moten, "Blackness and Nothingness (Mysticism in the Flesh)," *South Atlantic Quarterly* 12, no. 4 (2013), 746.

are always already piecing together a non-agential *poesis* or self-making—one that need not arrive at form, structure, or a wor(l)d.[42] The rest of us might learn from their example if we are to prepare our own house for the end of the world that is nothing short of the end of Man.

Jay-Z and Arthur Jafa gesture toward this non-agential living in the music video for "4:44," layering a critique of the human—exemplified by the black robot featured in minute 5:43—atop imagery about the possibilities of black femme(inist) bodily comportment—exemplified by the movements of Brooklyn-based performer and 2018 MacArthur genius Okwui Okpokwasili of—atop beats (in the music video, especially) that themselves "break," prolonged in the message (articulated in the lyrics to Jay-Z's title track) that love is the way out/through.[43]

Okpokwasili's movements—sharp and unanticipated—further impress the radical possibilities of breaking with Man's chronopolitical order to instead piece together non-agential *poesis*.

She moves not where she shouldn't but when she shouldn't, with a wilding imagination that is out of time, in no-time, in any time. Her improvisational getaway is "'[a] dance of body,'" "'[a] waltz of hips.'" Not an identity (arrival) but a praxis (departure), [she] "'turns/And … turns/And … turns,'" unfixing "all that we might place under the heading of time."

Positivism and progress—the promise of a "beyond"—are not hers to claim (they never were). Her unsanctioned movements built this "time of the now," "danc[ing] the beginning of humanity and the genesis of creativity," and she's "still fucking here," threading Man's timeline, skipping rocks across the coordinates of his *longue durée*.

Not anti-historical but ante-historical; not (just) paraontological but paralogical. Lawless. Mutinous. Insurgent. [She] does not wait for "cessation or interruption of historical flow" to "[move] 'to music not yet written.'" She goes mad and loses her mind to this song.

Her movements are "mad black," "mad queer," mad free, mad mad. Not doubly conscious (*pace* Du Bois) but cognitively dissonant (*pace* Fanon), [she] is "out of possession of [her] mind." She "dance[s] to 'the music of the madness'" because it's the only tune that's playing.

---

[42] See Alexis Pauline Gumbs, *M archive: After the end of the world* (Durham: Duke University Press, 2020).

[43] Fred Moten, *In the Break: The Aesthetics of the Black Radical Tradition* (University of Minnesota Press, 2003).

Insofar as Okpokwasili's movements are "mad black," she models the "black femme(inist) poethics" Denise Ferreira Da Silva describes: a self-making that is, as bell hooks writes, *all about love*.[44] Okpokwasili does as all black women do: she assembles her life-making in piecemeal, as a critical materialism that dispenses with the formal elements of language, like syntax and grammar, to create (not a world, that is to say, not a relationality, but) a sociality in which movement need not be constrained by the humanist (*qua* antiblack) mandates of *time*.

UPSETTING THE CARTESIAN DUALISM OF LIBERAL HUMANISM

4:44 demonstrates in words and images that racial blackness stands outside of and disrupts human recognition and protection, including their protracted possibilities in a post-human world. Specifically, the music video for the album's title track helps us to understand how the academy's discussion of the post-human re/produces the Cartesian dualism that pits mind against matter, and therefore, I want to argue, humanness (*qua* whiteness) against racial blackness. Within this binary model, black people can only ever occupy a negative term in the dialectic, as that matter which is "law-likely" subsumed by the rational mind. In "4:44," Jay-Z elaborates the self-discipline that makes matter (or, flesh) a prosthesis of the mind (*qua* body) as a *racial* violence. Which is to say, rather than disingenuously invoke the future-perfect tense of the post-human as a location in which black lives *can* matter, Jay-Z engages in a "discussion of the unthought," thinking with the figure of the post-human as an *anti-human* that is a critical materialism in the making of the human (*qua* whiteness). Unlike the recent scholarship on the post-human to emerge from femme(inist) science studies and similar (inter)disciplines, *this* thinking with the materiality of racial blackness—as a kind of assemblage—actually accounts for the racial making of who counts as human (or not).

As the black feminine-presenting robot in the music video for "4:44," shown intercepting a 1985 interview with Jean Michel Basquiat—in which he laments being made a spectacle by media reporters—bemoans, *"I am having an existential crisis here. Am I alive? Do I actually exist? Will I die?"* Not the post-human but some*thing* essentially divested of human

---

[44] See Ferreira da Silva, "Toward a Black Femme(inist) Poethics"; hooks, *All About Love: New Visions*.

recognitions and protections, the black person who is denied what Fanon describes as "onto-logical resistance," like Jay-Z's robot, experiences not just a closed door to relationality (i.e., to the world), but also and especially a portal into an/Other sociality: a cosmological Otherwise in which social life is constructed not from/as narrative coherence but in/as piecemeal.[45] This is an Otherwise defined not by continuity, but by the racialized cut, as exemplified by—not the smooth transitions between moving images and sounds in the music video for "4:44," but—the cuts that create narrative disjunctures and dehiscence, characteristic of Jafa's directorial style and Okpokwasili's dance aesthetic.

Indeed, Jay-Z's "post"-human is perhaps better understood as a materialism whereby the black person who is proscribed from the category of the human finds not narrative coherence—not a history or *her*-story (i.e., even an alternative dialectic) through which she can make meaning of her lived experiences—but its absence. That absence or lacuna is a *tabula rasa* in which black lives can matter, not least of all because the absence of a wor(l)d does not preclude the making and sustaining of (non-genealogical, or queer) ties that bind. I want to suggest that the cut that frames the robot's insight that she is the living dead, and the following clip—grainy footage of Al Green performing "Judy"—impart an important lesson: that the social life of social death is actualized as a *love praxis*.[46] Specifically, Green, who is shown singing the opening lyrics, "I never thought dreams could happen," followed by the refrain, "Since I met Judy," contextualizes the *mise-en-scène* of "4:44"—a music video which features moving images of antiblack violence at the same time as it includes images of a black love born (im/possibly) from the camera's racialized cut—as a location where *black freedom dreams* "could happen."

Specifically, the footage of Green is followed by moving images of Jay-Z and Beyoncè dancing on a concert stage together (also to "Judy"). In addition to advancing the idea that black love is a revolution/the revolution is black love, this clip, in which the Carters are shown courting each other in bodily comportment and movement—not as individuated bodies with impermeable boundaries, but rather, as flesh, which can be molded and melded and manipulated to fold into an/Other materialism—suggests a triumph of matter over mind. Indeed, the fact that Jay-Z and

---

[45] Fanon, *Black Skin, White Masks*, 110.

[46] See, Al Green, *Let's Stay Together*. 1972. Royal Recordings; hooks, *All About Love: New Visions*.

Beyoncè lean into each other (i.e., are pulled toward each other during the course of the dance), suggests that the matter that is black life can move on its own, independent of the rational mind that—as humanist lore would have us believe—puppeteers this (black) matter.

This sequence of clips constructs the message that black love is the antidote to the "existential crisis" that racial blackness—as a material assemblage—inaugurates, which is the crisis of *non-being*, or of absence. Recall that this is the same message advanced by the song's lyrics, which implore, "We're supposed to laugh 'til our heart stops/ And then meet in a space where the dark stop/*And let love light the way*." In these lyrics, and in the clip of Jay-Z and Beyoncè dancing on stage to "Judy"—a clip which materializes in/as narrative discontinuity, sandwiched between Al Green's performance of "Judy" and Beyoncè's performance of "All Night"—Jay-Z and Jafa construct the message that the im/possibility of black love materializes in the "break," that is to say, in the disjunctures and dehiscence that constitute a lacuna (though notably, not a landing) for the articulation of black life.[47]

What black love inaugurates, then, is a freedom that is yet to come and which has not yet arrived—indeed, I want to suggest, which necessarily cannot arrive but, when it does, will unfold (as) a feminine and feminized "excellence"—as Jay-Z elaborates in "Legacy," the album's final track, dedicated to his children—that will save us all, as black women and femmes have always done, so that "someday we'll all be free." To be sure, while the lesson that black love is a technology of the revolution/that the revolution is a technology of a "love ethic" is not necessarily afropessimism's insight, it is certainly a black femme(inist) argument, advanced by—among others—bell hooks, who concurs that there can be no justice without love, and no love without justice.[48]

UPSETTING THE TELEOLOGY OF LIBERAL HUMANISM

When paired with relevant scholarship, visual media as an allegory for humanist epistemology has made it possible for my students to query the race/ist workings of space, and especially, time. Jay-Z's *4:44*, especially, has prompted understanding of how space and time converge to make structure or form, or a container for being and doing and knowing (i.e.,

---

[47] Moten, *In the Break.*
[48] See hooks, *All About Love: New Visions.*

the human) that is expressly antiblack, insofar as the human's onto-epistemic order accumulates and makes-fungible (and feminine) black flesh as the raw material for its phallic wor(l)d-making. Visual media is thus effective insofar as it enables students to map "the world that the world lives in," acquiring tools to sabotage and radically upend this world without holding out hope for another world (or, word) that cannot but reproduce more of the present antiblackness in some future-perfect space-time; as in academic forays into the "post"-human that serve no purpose but to distract us from the project of complete and total liberation, of get-ting free from Man and his timeline.[49] The existential *qua* metaphysical crisis initiated by the problem of racial blackness and expressed by the robot *of color* in "4:44" underscores this.

The *poesis* or self-making—the "invention"—that will make black life matter requires not "post" humanism, but that we "leap" in this skin, with this flesh. Black freedom for afropessimism, as well as for the black femme(inist)s who underwrite afropessimism's critique, is a fugitive praxis that is about escape rather than arrival into new categories of order.[50] It is best articulated in/as *poesis* because poetic renderings abide by no formal structuring devices like grammar that force onto-epistemic order or wor(l)ding.

In calling for *poesis*, then, black invention wants us to feel "freer than we want to be."[51] It wants a gratuitous freedom that "can be felt and per-ceived even though—or especially if—it remains unrecognizable to our current common senses."[52] It seeks not world-making but a cosmology or sociality, indeed, an *ecology* in which life matters independent of any "attempts to contain it," which might "include processes or recognition, narrative, and other formal devices."[53]

By clarifying this Otherwise as a "leaping," in other words, as a grasp-ing for and inching toward, rather than as an arrival or landing or *telos*, students understand how social life inheres in/as the survival dance and sorrow song of social death.[54] The black femme(inist) futurity that under-writes afropessimism's critique and Jay-Z's success is a liberatory moment

---

[49] Sexton, "The Social Life of Social Death," 28.
[50] Fanon, *Black Skin, White Masks*, 229.
[51] Marquis Bey, *Black Trans Feminist* (Durham: Duke University Press, 2022), 227.
[52] Kara Keeling, "Looking for M—Queer Temporality, Black Political Possibility, and Poetry from the Future," *GLQ: A Journal of Lesbian and Gay Studies* 15, no. 4 (2009): 567.
[53] Keeling, "Looking for M—Queer Temporality," 567.
[54] Fanon, *Black Skin, White Masks*, 229.

that does not arrive—that cannot arrive—but which also *cannot stop arriving*.[55] Accordingly, Alexis Pauline Gumbs describes the work of black femme(inism)s as "the experimental creation of a rival economy *and temporality* in which Black women and children [are] generators of an alternative destiny."[56]

In this alternative timeline (that is no timeline at all, insofar as it does not arrive or land), the lives of black women and femmes who are the generators of life matter first/last/only, and in doing so, create the conditions of possibility for all historical-racial, sex and gender, and sectarian differences—for example, as Jay-Z enumerates them in the song "Legacy": Muslim, Buddhist, and Christian—to inhere value. This is what it means to inhabit the "break" of Jay-Z's songwriting: "a space where the dark stops" and (black) love instead "lights the way," toward a temporal arrangement in which "we'll all be free."[57]

BEYOND THE CLASSROOM: A FEMME(INIST) *MOVEMENT*

Afropessimism recognizes that liberalism's capaciousness—its increasingly widening circle of inclusion—only ever expands (e.g., in the service of multiculturalism) in order to contract; in the end, excluding racial blackness, using black abjection as the foil to everyone else's inclusion in the liberal project. More to the point, as an avowed black femme(inist) project, afropessimism understands that as hyper-penetrable Others, racially black persons are the personification of "female flesh ungendered," and that as an un/gendered assemblage of flesh, racial blackness defaults to the feminine/feminized position, making all black life femme life, and making gender a race problem.[58]

In Arthur Jafa's care, the music video to Jay-Z's "4:44" provides an opportunity for thinking about un/gendered flesh as the "effeminacy" of racial blackness.[59] The video borrows its collage style from Jafa's *Love is the Message, The Message is Death* and includes personal sightings of Spillers (at

---

[55] This moment that does not/cannot arrive and which does not stop arriving is a symptom of what David Marriott describes as the future-*imperfect* tense. Marriott reflects that the "destination" of the future-imperfect moment—of black liberation—"cannot be foreseen, or anticipated, but only repeatedly, traveled" (Marriott 2011, 53–54).
[56] Gumbs, "m/other ourselves," 21. Emphasis added.
[57] See Moten, *In the Break*.
[58] Spillers, "Mama's Baby, Papa's Maybe."
[59] See Gordon, *Bad Faith and Antiblack Racism*.

minute mark 5:05) and Saidiya Hartman (at minute mark 2:29).[60] Not only are Spillers' and Hartman's persons cited, but their corpus is taken up in movement, too, notably, in conversation with Okpokwasili's choreographed stylings. Her dance praxis generativity engages their black femme(inist) scholarship[61] to imagine the pain, pleasure, and im/possibility of racial blackness in bodily comportment, in and as a disjointed and disorderly black femme(inist) movement, as a kind of "anarchy" in which black women and femmes "assemble in a riotous manner" to create an "[irrupt] the fabric of existence."[62]

In the video for "4:44," Okpokwasili dances frantically and fervently, with sharp movements, to embody "'the music of the madness'" that is the lie of a universal humanism.[63] To dance in this way, in a way that creates frenetic distress, without advancing in any direction, is to lean into "[the] madness within," which is also or primarily about the madness without, and about the temporal death that humanism assigns to racial blackness.[64]

Likewise, Beyoncè and the woman and femmes who appears with her in *Lemonade* express the pain and pleasure of racial blackness in/as bodily movement, in other words, in/as a black femme(inist) comportment. Their gestures—disjointed and fractured, constitutive not of a whole but of traces, performed during the album's interludes and breaks, contributing not to the narrative coherence of lyricism but to its dehiscence—*birth* Jay-Z's interventions in *4:44*, evident not just in the visual album, but in his own embodied relationship to the music.

To engage the quest(ion) of black femme(inism)s in/as *movement*, my students considered not just Jay-Z's lyricism and imagery, but also how his own body unfolded at a December 2017 concert in Chicago. They queried how he curated movement more generally, for example, on set, noting that the concert stage was made up of large, movable screens that displayed live close-ups of some of Jay-Z's most iconic gestures, as well as

[60] Arthur Jafa, "Love Is the Message, the Message Is Death." *Los Angeles: Museum of Contemporary Art* (2017). Both clips of Hortense Spillers and Saidiya Hartman originally appear in Arthur Jafa's *Dreams Are Colder than Death*. 2013. Pumpernickel Films.

[61] See Andrew Rossi's 2017 documentary on Okwui Okpokwasili's creative process, entitled *Bronx Gothic*. 2017. Grasshopper Film.

[62] See Saidiya Hartman, "The Anarchy of Colored Girls Assembled in a Riotous Manner," *South Atlantic Quarterly* 177, no. 3 (2018); Bey, *Black Trans Feminist*, 150.

[63] Sexton, "The Social Life of Social Death," 6.

[64] Sexton, "The Social Life of Social Death," 6.

grainy VHS footage that unfolded frantically, over and on top of one another, to deliver a message about social life that cuts through the continuum of space and time.

Students noted that Jay-Z's movements at the concert—dubbed on large, mobile screens to appear not in-sync with the live performance but *out-of-time*—functioned as a kind of black *poesis*. They reflected that in Jay-Z's frenetic Otherwise, black life, which for Jay-Z—an artist prolific in his responses to structural antiblackness—has always been about "the streets," creates its own meaning, irrespective of the expressed interests of the (white) symbolic order.

As Frantz Fanon enumerates in his clinical research, especially, in descriptions of "existing triply,"[65] and as emergent scholarship in performance studies and at the intersection of drama theory and black study aver,[66] the body's comportment is a master code for how racial blackness articulates inside or outside of (or under) space and time, occupying not "the time of the now"[67] or even the same timeline as "the now" but a nowhere or "sunken place"[68] in which the black person is alienated

---

[65] Fanon in *Black Skin, White Masks*, describes "existing triply," as the cognitive dissonance of existing outside the self, writing, "The white man [...] had woven me out of a thousand details, anecdotes, stories. ... 'Look, a Negro!' It was an external stimulus that flicked over me as I passed by. I made a tight smile. 'Look, a Negro!' It was true. It amused me. 'Look, a Negro!' The circle was drawing a bi tighter. I made no secret of my amusement. 'Mama, see the Negro! I'm frightened!' Frightened! Frightened! Now they were beginning to be afraid of me. I made up my mind to laugh myself to tears, but laughter had become impossible. I could no longer laugh, because I already knew that there were legends, stories, history, and above all *historicity*. ... In the train it was no longer a question of being aware of my body in the third person but in a triple person. In the train I was given not one but two, three places. ... I existed triply: I occupied space [but not time]. ... I was responsible at the same time for my body, for my race, for my ancestors. I subjected myself to an objective examination, I discovered by blackness, my ethnic characteristics; and I was battered down by tom-toms, cannibalism, intellectual deficiency, fetishism, racial defects, slave-ships, and above all else, above all: 'Sho' good eatin'" (Fanon 1986, 111–112).

[66] See Jaye Austin Williams, "Radical Black Drama-as-Theory: The Black Femme(inist) Dramatic on the Protracted Event-Horizon," *Theory & Event* 21, no. 1 (January 2018): 191–214.; and Jeramy DeCristo, "Music Against the Subject," *Theory & Event* 21, no. 1 (January 2018): 169–190.

[67] See Walter Benjamin, "Theses on the Philosophy of History," *Illuminations* (Schocken Books, 1968). This is Walter Benjamin's term for "empty homogenous time": a "constellation of the past and present" that induces "'the time of the now'"—that is, of modernity—as Western Europe's present/now. In this context, non-Western European actors are always already belated (1968, 253–264).

[68] Jordan Peele, "Get Out" (Universal Pictures, 2017).

even (especially) from her own bodily movements.[69] Thus, what students observed at the concert—a kind of out-of-sync-ness—signals social death (i.e., stasis) as much as it gestures toward a different, non-agential social life or *poesis* (i.e., non-directional movement).

MAKING *LEMONADE* FROM LEMONS: THE BLACK, FEMININE SOCIAL LIFE OF BLACK SOCIAL DEATH

Jay-Z's intervention is inconceivable without the cosmological Otherwise that Beyoncè introduces in *Lemonade*. While both *4:4* and *Lemonade* reflect ~~afropessimism's~~ black femme(inism)'s demand that we think seek to understand how social life inheres not in spite of, but in/as/through social death—that black life *can* matter Otherwise because it *cannot* matter in humanist or historical terms—and further, while both albums impress that is black women and femmes who do the difficult work of making ~~black~~ all life matter (not in spite of these odds, but in/as/through these odds), it is Beyoncè's album and not Jay-Z's that exemplifies what the "elsewhere and elsewhen" in which black (women's and femmes') freedom is prioritized over and against all other freedoms, looks and feels like.[70]

We see that black fugitivity is an ~~afropessimistic~~ black femme(inist) project most clearly in *Lemonade*'s interludes, specifically, in scenes that submerge Beyoncè and the black women and femmes she appears with in water. The pairing of these scenes—not (just) of subjection, but also, of liberation—with critiques, for example, of slavery's water politics, offered

---

[69] This in/ability to move—not just metaphysically, in other words, not just when black people are the "zero degree" (Spillers 1987, 67) of the progress narrative that is human (his) story, but also and especially in/as habitus and corporeal operations—is what Fanon gestures toward when he writes about the lived experience of "existing triply." He explains, "In the white world, the man of color encounters difficulties in the development of his bodily schema. Consciousness of the body is solely a negating activity. It is a third-person consciousness. The body is surrounded by an atmosphere of certain uncertainty. I know that if I want to smoke, I shall have to reach out my right arm and take the pack of cigarettes lying at the other end of the table, and I shall have to lean back slightly. And all of these movements are made not out of habit but out of implicit knowledge. A slow composition of my *self* as a body in the middle of a spatial and temporal world—such seems to be the schema. It does not impose itself on me; it is, rather, a definitive structuring of the self and the world—definitive because it creates a real dialectic between my body and the world" (1986, 110–111).

[70] Moten, "Blackness and Nothingness," 746.

by Christina Sharpe and M. Nourbese Philip,[71] ushers students to con-sider how and why black life is most liberatory when it is "lived under-ground, in outer space"—or underwater, as it were.[72] As one student reflects,

> *Lemonade* creates a space of black social life when Beyoncè dives from the roof and becomes submerged in water. The visual album seems to suggest that the space of underwater can function metaphorically similarly to Sexton's location of social life underground and/or in outer space. For black social life to exist, there must be a departure from our current universe and its inherently anti-black production of knowledge. Beyoncè positions underwater as a space in which black bodies are freed from their static teleo-logical position and are granted mobility. Different rules govern the move-ment of a body underwater and Lemonade highlights this in the scene immediately following her dive from the roof, where Beyoncè exists in a bedroom entirely filled with water, with disruptions in time (movements showed in reverse, sped up, etc.) and the inclusion of movement impossible outside of water (floating, breath manifesting itself as bubbles, etc.). To me, this scene grounds the entire rest of the album within an underwater world. In this world, straightjackets become, not immobilizing, but a means of connection between dancing women in a parking lot (traditionally also a place of immobility). This universe arms Beyoncè with a bat to smash the panopticon embodied by the camera, reminding the viewer that despite the possibilities offered by the world of *Lemonade* we are still viewing it and processing it through an anti-black [*sic*] lens and until we ourselves access a new world and new process of knowledge production (through madness, neurosis, flight) a true understanding of Beyoncè's fantasy is impossible.

Absent the critical interventions of afropessimism's black femme(inism)s, stated another way, absent the critical intervention of *4:44*'s predecessor, *Lemonade,* Beyoncè's album, like Jay-Z's *4:44*, is decipherable only in symbolic terms; for example—in Beyoncè's case—as evidence (enough) of "black girl magic," without a real understanding of what that magic looks like or why the social life black women create is always already Otherworldly. Returning afropessimism to the black femme(inist) citations of its ances-tors, m/others, and aunties encourages students to instead engage with the material as a structural critique, specifically, as a critique of the

[71] See Sharpe, *In the Wake*; M. Nourbese Philip. *Zong!* (Middletown: Wesleyan University Press, 2011).
[72] Sexton, "The Social Life of Social Death," 28.

relationship between space, time, and ontological im/possibility; and to ask questions like, *Why the water? Why the foliage? Is that a plantation I'm seeing?*

While Jay-Z's *4:44* curates movement in sound and image to stage a metaphysical intervention that interrogates space and time *as form*, encouraging students to (re)think the onto-epistemic order of patriarchy as a symptom not of white supremacy, but rather, of antiblackness; it is Beyoncè and the women and femmes she appears with in *Lemonade* (and not Jay-Z)—much like the women and femmes who galvanize afropessimism's critique—who have taught my students what the Otherwise that Jay-Z (like afropessimism) gestures toward might look like. These black femme(inist) citations change students' *scale* of analysis from questions of identity and difference—an analytic orientation that can only ever think about "the transparent I" and its attendant forms of mastery and agency, in other words, antiblackness—to questions of structure and power, which are essentially black femme(inist) questions about being and non-being.[73] Rather than take identity and difference for granted as stable categories, the latter approach queries how these assemblages cohere (or don't).

Absent these citations, students would not know how to conceptualize the *poesis* that Frantz Fanon's call a black "invention" and which afropessimism tells us will destabilize the liberal humanist arrangement of space and time that is responsible for black social death.[74] As we engage afropessimism's critique in increasingly populist terms, we would be wise to remember that even Jay-Z knows where his bread is buttered. Black women and femmes have always done the difficult, unglamorous, and unrecognized work of birthing and sustaining not just black life, but *all life*, as the "custodians" of our collective, coalitional "house of resistance."[75]

BIBLIOGRAPHY

Benjamin, Walter. *Illuminations.* New York: Schocken Books, 1968.
Bey, Marquis. *Black Trans Feminist.* Durham: Duke University Press, 2022.
Brand, Dionne. *A map to the door of no return: Notes to belonging.* Toronto: Vintage Canada, 2002.

---

[73] See Denise Ferreira Da Silva, *Towards a Global Idea of Race* (Minneapolis: University of Minnesota Press, 2007).

[74] Fanon, *Black Skin, White Masks*, 229.

[75] Davis, "Reflections on the Black Woman's Role in the Community of Slaves," 89.

Combahee River Collective, "A Black Feminist Statement," *Home Girls, A Black Feminist Anthology*, ed. Barbara Smith. 210-218. New York: Kitchen Table: Women of Color Press, Inc., 1983.

Da Silva, Denise Ferreira. *Towards a Global Idea of Race*. Minneapolis: University of Minnesota Press, 2007.

Da Silva. "Toward a black feminist poethics: The quest (ion) of blackness toward the end of the world." *The Black Scholar* 44, no. 2 (2014): 81-97.

Davis, Angela. "Reflections on the Black Woman's Role in the Community of Slaves." *The Massachusetts Review* 13, no. 1/2 (1972): 81-100.

DeCristo, Jeramy. "Music against the subject." *Theory & Event* 21, no. 1 (2018): 169-190.

Fanon, Frantz. *Black Skin, White Masks*, trans. Charles Lam Markmann. London: Pluto Press, 1986.

Gordon, Lewis R. *Bad Faith and Antiblack Racism*. New York: Humanities Press International, 1995.

Gumbs, Alexis Pauline. "m/other ourselves: a Black queer femme(inist) genealogy for radical mothering." In *Revolutionary Mothering: Love on the Front Lines*, ed. Alexis Pauline Gumbs, China Martens and Mai'a Williams. Binghamton, NY: PM Press 2016.

———. *M archive: After the end of the world*. Duke University Press, 2020.

Hartman, Saidiya. *Scenes of Subjection: Terror, Slavery, and Self-Making in Nineteenth-Century America*. New York: Oxford University Press, 1997.

———. *Lose Your Mother: A Journey Along the Atlantic Slave Route*. New York: Farrar, Straus and Giroux 2007.

———. "The anarchy of colored girls assembled in a riotous manner." *South Atlantic Quarterly* 117, no. 3 (2018): 465-490.

hooks, bell. *Black Looks: Race and Representation*. Boston: South End Press 1992.

———. *All About Love: New Visions*. New York: William Morrow Paperback, 2018.

Iasimone, Ashley. "Jay-Z's Shawn Carter Foundation Raises $20 Million at 20th Anniversary Gala in New York." *Billboard*, July 15, 2023.

Jafa, Arthur. *Dreams Are Colder than Death*. 2013. Pumpernickel Films.

———. "Love Is the Message, the Message Is Death." *Los Angeles: Museum of Contemporary Art* (2017).

Keeling, Kara. "LOOKING FOR M—Queer Temporality, Black Political Possibility, and Poetry from the Future." *GLQ: A Journal of Lesbian and Gay Studies* 15, no. 4 (2009): 565-582.

Kendall, Mikki. "bell hooks pushed us to think harder about feminism, Black women and Beyonce." *The Washington Post*, December 16, 2021.

Lemieux, Jamilah. "Stop Trying to Be Good—Be Black." *Mic* (June 30, 2015).

Lorde, Audre. "Age, Race, Class, and Sex: Women Redefining Difference," in *Sister Outsider: Essays and Speeches by Audre Lorde*. Berkeley: Crossing Press 2007.

Lyotard, Jean-Francois. *Libidinal Economy*, trans. Iain Hamilton Grant. Bloomington: Indiana University Press, 1993.

Malaklou, M. Shadee. "'Teaching Trayvon' at Irvine: On Femme(inist) Praxis, Afro-pessimism, and 'Woke Work.'" *National Political Science Review* 18 (December 2016), n.p.

Marriott, David. "Inventions of Existence: Sylvia Wynter, Frantz Fanon, Sociogeny, and" the Damned"." *CR: The New Centennial Review* 11, no. 3 (2011): 45-89.

Montgomery, Sarah Jasmine. "Jay-Z's 40/40 Club is hosting a fundraiser to help Puerto Rico," *Fader*, October 4, 2017.

Moten, Fred. *In the Break: The Aesthetics of the Black Radical Tradition*. Minneapolis: University of Minnesota Press, 2003.

———. "Blackness and nothingness (mysticism in the flesh)." *South Atlantic Quarterly* 112, no. 4 (2013): 737-780.

Peele, Jordan. *Get Out*. 2017. Universal Pictures.

Philip, M. NourbeSe. *Zong!* Middletown: Wesleyan University Press, 2011.

Rossi. Andrew. *Bronx Gothic*. 2017. Grasshopper Film.

Sexton, Jared. "The Social Life of Social Death: On Afro-Pessimism and Black Optimism," *InTensions* 5 (Fall/Winter 2011): 1-47. https://intensions.journals.yorku.ca/index.php/intensions/article/view/37359

Sharpe, Christina. *In the Wake: On Blackness and Being*. Durham: Duke University Press, 2016.

Spillers, Hortense. "Mama's Baby, Papa's Maybe: An American Grammar Book." *Diacritics* 17, no. 2 (1987): 64-81.

Wilderson III, Frank B. *Red, White & Black: Cinema and the Structure of U.S. Antagonisms*. Durham: Duke University Press, 2010.

———. *Afropessimism*. New York: Liveright, 2020.

Wilderson III, Frank B., and Shannon Walsh, "Afro-pessimism and Friendship in South Africa: An Interview with Frank B. Wilderson III." In *Ties that Bind: Race and the Politics of Friendship in South Africa*, ed. Shannon Walsh and John Soske. 70-99. Johannesburg: Wits University Press, 2016.

Williams, Jaye Austin. "Radical black drama-as-theory: The black feminist dramatic on the protracted event-horizon." *Theory & Event* 21, no. 1 (2018): 191-214.

Williams, John. "In 'Afropessimism,' a Black Intellectual Mixes Memoir and Theory." *The New York Times*, April 5, 2020.

Williams, Raymond and Michael Orrom. *Preface to Film*. London: Film Drama Limited, 1954.

Wynter, S., and K. McKittrick. "Unparalleled catastrophe for our species? Or, to give humanness a different future: Conversations." In K. McKittrick, ed. *Sylvia Wynter: On being human as praxis*. 9–89. Durham: Duke University Press, 2015.

DISCOGRAPHY

Beyonce. *Lemonade*. 2016. Parkwood Entertainment.
Green, Al. *Let's Stay Together*. 1972. Royal Recordings.
Jay Z. *4:44*, 2017. Roc Nation.
Simone, Nina. *Wild as the Wind*. 1966. Philips.

Toward a [Black] Hip Hop Aesthetic: Against Manifestations of the Neoliberal Universal (A Percussive Manifesto of Sorts)

Wind Dell Woods

Hip hop seems to be everywhere; let me repeat and revise, the siphoning and redeploying of its most marketable element, rap, occurs in a host of divergent locations, from political campaigns to college classrooms, from Disney films to Broadway stages. Rap, though often met with a phobic response when associated with black youth, becomes the ideal seasoning to add a little edge to any lackluster project[1]: Need to get "at-risk youth"

---

[1] I am of course thinking of bell hooks's *Black Looks: Race and Representation* (Boston: South End Press, 1992) when she states "Within commodity culture, ethnicity becomes spice, seasoning that can liven up the dull dish that is mainstream white culture," (21). I also want layer on hooks's assertion a few samples: first, what has been called the "loud music murder case" of Jordan Davis in Florida (https://www.floridatoday.com/story/news/crime/2016/11/17/michael-dunn-murder-conviction-upheld-loud-music-fatal-shooting/94019188/); second, the stabbing of Elijah Al-Amin in Arizona (https://abcnews.go.com/US/arizona-man-killed-teen-rap-music-made-feel/story?id=64207831); third, the

---

W. D. Woods (✉)
University of Puget Sound, Department of Theatre Arts, Tacoma, WA, USA
e-mail: wwoods@pugetsound.edu

© The Author(s), under exclusive license to Springer Nature Switzerland AG 2025
P. K. Saucier (ed.), *Critical Essays on Hip Hop and the Study of Hip Hop*, https://doi.org/10.1007/978-3-031-80763-3_5

91

to attend your outdated theater season? Sprinkle a little hip hop on it. Need to give your syllabus a little bit of *flava*? Add a dash of Rap. Need to radicalize your pedagogy? Infuse your curriculum with overblown claims of structural transformation by way of performative stylization. After all, the hydraulics of oppression are something that one can pop and lock their way out of.[2] But be careful. There are rules to this… One being, never use hip hop uncut or in the raw. It must be diluted with lukewarm water from the mainstream. If need be, say you are "elevating" it to the realm of "legitimate" art, poetry, or an authentic cultural tradition, so it (but not its burdens) belongs to everyone.[3] If hip hop is still not *fungible* enough for your taste, position multicultural and (neo)liberal theories as the only valid frames of analysis for hip hop while at the same time policing and invalidating hip hop's (own) hermeneutics.[4] Follow these rules and you will have the perfect additive for any endeavor that is unwilling to address the demands of black people "in and against the [antiblack] world," or

shooting of Aidan Ellison in Ashland, Oregon (https://www.npr.org/2020/12/04/942946598/oregon-town-grapples-with-shooting-death-of-19-year-old-aidan-ellison); and finally, a "primal scene" described by Sharon P. Holland in "The Question of Normal." *GLQ: A Journal of Lesbian and Gay Studies* 10, no. 1 (2003): 128–131. Where the first three "events" are easily discernible in their antiblackness. A white man murders a black teenage over his music, the fourth one speaks to the sonic offense and antagonism that even so-called well-meaning white people have toward hip hop when in proximity to black bodies.

[2] I'm echoing a similar problematic that P. Khalil Saucier and Tryon Woods identify in their chapter "Against hip hop Studies." There, they point to what they find as an "overemphasis on the conception of racism as performance—the *doing* of repression and resistance" in which "hip hop [is] construed by educators and scholars in its liberatory guise: hip hop culture, according to this line of thought, offers a way out of the alienation of racism and late capitalism" (Saucier and Woods 2015, 158).

[3] I am sampling the title from Greg Tate's book *Everything but the Burden: What White People are Taking from Black Culture* (New York: Broadway Books, 2003).

[4] Tricia Rose states in the Epilogue to her groundbreaking and genre-defining book *Black Noise: Rap Music and Black Culture in Contemporary America* (Middletown: Wesleyan University Press, 1994), that "although rappers are some of the most prominent social critics in contemporary popular culture, they remain some of the most intuitionally policed and stigmatized" (184). I want to cite and, slightly, revise this sample by highlighting the fact that rappers are not solely policed and stigmatized for being rappers, but this disciplinary overseeing has also to do with the tradition of Black political thought that many rappers educe and extend in their lyrics. In other words, it is a combination of a "Fear of a Black Planet" (and the power to give that fear objective value) and the rhymes and reasons that rappers assert in and against an antiblack world.

even better, directly works against those very demands.[5] If hip hop is everywhere, it is because there is currency, as well as creative and political energy, to be siphoned, tapped like crude oil from (the) underground. This chapter takes up the questions: if hip hop is one of the only spaces on the planet where a wide spectrum of people come together to think, create, and be in and through an unarguably black aesthetic and expressive tradition, why do many of the projects that emerge out of these spaces so often ignore black suffering and leave the demands of *black noise* unheard?[6] How is hip hop employed in these projects to animate some agendas while undermining others? To spin it a bit differently but still in the same groove, how is hip hop redeployed "across an astonishing diversity of political, economic, and cultural conjunctions"[7] to render black people "refugees in everyone else's political project."[8]

Originally, this chapter was centered on Lin-Manuel Miranda's musical *Hamilton*. I have chosen to decenter *Hamilton* and interrogate the troubling questions posed above from a different vantage. Although *Hamilton* provides ample illustrations of the problematics I want to uncover, I want to broaden my argument and extend my critique beyond one sample in order to suggest that there is a deeper and more pervasive issue at hand.[9]

---

[5] Two points: first, the phrasing "in and against the world" comes from a lecture titled "Hesitant Sociology: Blackness in Poetry" by Fred Moten. Second, for a different spin—yet still in the same groove—of my argument about the cooptation of black energy to fuel a non-black (or even antiblack) agenda see Jared Sexton, *Amalgamation Schemes: Antiblackness and the Critique of Multiracialism* (Minneapolis: University of Minnesota Press, 2008); P. Khalil Saucier and Tryon Woods, "Hip Hop Studies in Black." *Journal of Popular Music Studies* 26, no 2–3 (2014): 268–294; Frank B. Wilderson III, *Red, White & Black: Cinema and the Structure of U.S. Antagonisms* (Durham: Duke University Press, 2010); Sylvia Wynter, *Do Not Call Us Negros: How "Multicultural" Textbooks Perpetuate Racism* (San Francisco: Aspire Books, 1990).

[6] I am thinking, here, of two specific references: First, Tricia Rose's *Black Noise* and Saidiya Hartman's formulation of black noise in "Venus in Two Acts." *Small Axe* 12, no. 2 (2008): 1–14. There, Hartman writes: "black noise—the shrieks, the moans, the nonsense, and the opacity, which are always in excess of legibility and of the law and which hint at and embody aspirations that are wildly utopian, derelict to capitalism, and antithetical to its attendant discourse of Man" (12).

[7] Saucier and Woods, "Hip Hop Studies in Black," 268.

[8] Frank B. Wilderson III, *Afropessimism* (New York: Liveright, 2020), 28.

[9] The musical *Hamilton* is still dis-cussed in this essay through critical sampling. It will remain more in the background; however, it will, no doubt, haunt from the shadows of the thrust of this essay, perhaps, in a way not unlike the black ethical demands haunt from within the performance and dramaturgy of *Hamilton* itself.

Rather than analyze the limitations of one project to get at my claims, I make two critical cuts: First, I describe what I view as an ethical employment of hip hop aesthetics in theater through a concept I call *percussive dramaturgy*. This section is poly-voiced in that while describing and calling for a method(ology), I offer critical love (though it's a thin line between), in the form of riffs and ruptures, targeted at projects, approaches, and agendas that I find are, at best, sorely limited in their ability to tarry with the facts of (anti)blackness and, at worse, axiomatically antiblack themselves.[10]

The second cut engages in an analysis of playwright Rickerby Hinds's hip hop theater piece *Dreamscape* (2007) in order to further elucidate on the power and potential of percussive dramaturgy. Here, I track the ways in which Hinds uses hip hop aesthetics to remix (cite and revise) the real-life 1998 police shooting of Tyisha Miller in Riverside, California. Hinds's hip hop dramaturgy, rather than becoming enticed by the spectacular nature of performative violence targeted at black bodies or the performativity of resistance and redress—representational and thematic tropes that tend to saturate hip hop Theatre—ratchets up the level of abstraction and allows space to meditate on both performative and structural violence that inundates black (social) life *and* (social) death, as well as black (social) life *in and against*, (social) death, as Jared Sexton might have it.[11] Unlike the projects and approaches I reference in the first cut, Hinds's hip hop dramaturgy: (a) forces the audience to look *with* blackness, rather than, solely, look *at* black people and (b) generates percussive dissonance in which hip hop's black noise is brought into sonic relief.

---

[10] Jared Sexton says as much of Multiracial Studies in a lecture available on YouTube. There, he defines Multiracial Studies as "axiomatically anti-black which is to say at the level of its guiding assumptions and premises." See "What's Radical About 'Mixed Race'?," (https://www.youtube.com/watch?v=jSMQpRzcGpA).

[11] Sexton writes in "The Social Life of Social Death: On Afro-Pessimism and Black Optimism," *In Tensions Journal*, issue 5 (2011), n.p. that "To speak of black social life *and* black social death, black social life *against* black social death, black social life as black social death, black social life in black social death—all of this is to find oneself in the midst of an argument that is also a profound agreement, an agreement that takes shape in (between) *meconnaissance* and (dis)belief. Black optimism is not the negation of the negation that is afro-pessimism, just as black social life does not negate black social death by vitalizing it" (Sexton 2011).

CUT 1: THE PERCUSSIVE GENERATIVITY OF BLACK NOISE, A MANIFESTO (OF SORTS)

The paradox here, however, was that despite the widespread popular
dynamic of the Black Arts and Black Aesthetic Movements, they disap-
peared as if they had never been.
—Sylvia Wynter[12]

They have always tried to erase the Black presence from whatever
Black thing They took a shine to: jazz, blues, rock and roll, doowop,
swing dancing, cornrowing, anti-disimanation (sic) politics,
attacking Dead Men, you name it.
—Greg Tate[13]

This ghost town was once rare grooves and shattered snare drums
Cramped basement jams, suburbia wouldn't dare come
The death of an era gave birth to a phase
Frantic crowd calling "nigga" till we surrendered the trade
(Nigga?)
Now 'who stole the soul' became the phrase
When only eight niggas at the show and six of 'em is on stage.
—Lifesavas[14]

The 1986 documentary *Big Fun in the Big Town* contains a scene with
DJ legend and hip hop pioneer Grandmaster Flash describing the technique and philosophy of turntablism. Standing behind a mixer, two turntables (decks) on each side, Flash announces that he will "take [the record]
apart and put it back together." The record that he references is Bob
James's *Two* (1973). Duplicate copies of the same album lay on each of the
turntables. Flash commences to cut and scratch over (and through) the
two records, putting them into a type of percussive *dialectic*.[15]

---

[12] Sylvia Wynter, "On How We Mistook the Map for the Territory, and Reimprisoned
Ourselves in Our Unbearable Wrongness of Being, of *Desêtre*: Black Studies Toward the
Human Project,"in *Not Only the Master's Tools: African American Studies in Theory and
Practice*, eds. Lewis Gordon and Jane Anna Gordon, (New York: Routledge, 2006), 109.

[13] Tate, *Everything but the Burden*, 2.

[14] Lifesavas. "Skeletons," *Spirit in Stone*. Quannum Projects, 2003. CD.

[15] By dialectic, I do mean to evoke (most specifically) Hegel; however, I want to—as the
term *percussive* suggests—rhythmically educe and extend Hegel's concept. It is important to

Flash's apt description of his DJing technique—taking a record apart and putting it back together—is significant, I argue, because it speaks to hip hop's tendency to reference and revise the objects it encounters through a generative gesture called the "dis."[16] The dis is citational and re-creational move which renders the original "inadequate yet necessary" (as Derrida might have it).[17] What Flash testifies to is the fact that though a record is often imagined to be a sealed, complete, and closed off object, hip hop allows for a type of reopening. In the space of this rupture, in the cut, the break, reconstructive-cum-deconstructive possibilities emerge. In hip hop, the record is both played and played upon, rotating with possibility; in other words, in hip hop "the vinyl ain't [ever] final"; rather, it remains in dialectical dis-cussion.[18]

A record, here, can refer to anything: a vinyl disc with grooves, a public wall, a piano riff, a dance move, or a James Brown horn sample. But for this cut, records refer to dramatic works, and my aim is to: (a) set forth a hip hop dramaturgy situated in the continuum of, what Wynter has defined above as, the "Black Arts and Black Aesthetic Movements," a dramaturgy which works to elucidate "Black presence" rather than "erase it" (Tate's

---

note that my notion of percussivity, here, does not gesture toward a harmonious closer; rather, it encourages continuous rupture, repetitious sampling, and cutting. In other words, rather than think in terms of the traditional Hegelian triadic: thesis, antithesis, synthesis or problem, reaction, solution, I want to leave open the third step. In the place of "resolution," I am interested in a space of repetition and revision and continuous play.

[16] The use of the "dis" here extends from my work on *disaesthetics*. In short, disaesthetics is the writing over and through an original object, for example, when a graffiti writer approaches a "public" wall (the original) and tags or bombs it (the dis). To this "original" dis, another writer may go up over the "first" creating a palimpsestic reworking of space and meaning. The dis is also employed in rapping and rhyming when an emcee uses a lyric from another rapper, citing and rewriting it through a type of lyrical upcycling. Finally, the dis employs all the implications evoked by "dis-" as a prefix, in that it critically *dis*rupts, *dis*turbs, *dis*orders, *dis*regards, *dis*plays, *dis*orients, and so on.

[17] This phrase refers to Derrida's (by way of Heidegger's) concept of *sous rature* or "under erasure." See Jacques Derrida, *Of Grammatology* (Baltimore: The Johns Hopkins University Press, 1977), xvi; Madan Sarup, *An Introductory Guide to Post-structuralism and Postmodernism* (Longman, 1993), 33.

[18] The vinyl ain't final refers to hip hop's tendency to take apart and put back together the original record. It also references a phrase that a DJ might say at the end of an evening of rocking a party. In this case the meaning is, though the music is over (the last record has been played) the spirit continues. See Dipannita Basu, and Sidney J. Lemelle, eds. *The Vinyl Ain't Final: Hip Hop and the Globalization of Black Popular Culture.* (Ann Arbor: Pluto Press, 2006), 1.

epigraph); and (b) outline a hip hop hermeneutics which listens to (and for) the "rare grooves and shattered snare drums" of black noise. To do so, it is necessary to move beyond the politics of representation, (neo) liberal notions of diversity and inclusion, hyper-romanticized conceptions that suggest art can remedy all social ills, and sentimental and narrow portrayals of black achievement. In cutting up, into, and through, the records, this dramaturgical approach engages in a percussive encounter with dominant orders of knowledge, specifically those promoting liberal universal ideals that many hold so dear.

Riff/Rupture 1: Check(ing) the Method(olodgy)

By mobilizing rhythms across the communication landscape, the Rhythmengine
   crosspollinates the eager fan, transmaterializes your sensorium through the
   onomatopoeic illogic called HipHop.
—Kodwo Eshun[19]

[W]hat concerns me, as a dramaturg, is how to bring that which
   must be thought to rupture the rationalized political and aesthetic
   consensus, to contest what the dominant discourses assert as the
   illusion of the unthinkable.
—Hana Worthen[20]

Before I lay the tracks of my aim and analysis, I find it necessary to define my terms.

First, dramaturgy, here, refers to the art of playwriting (the craft of the dramatist), as well as the research and thinking that goes into producing a piece of theater. The former speaks to how the playwright constructs a play and thinks with(in) it (a playwright's dramaturgy), the latter describes the *study* of dramatic elements and how they function in the process of staging a play (production dramaturgy). Hana Worthen's description of the role of the dramaturg, as one that, "enunciates an understanding of theatre, an understanding of performance, and understanding of the ways

---

[19] Kodwo Eshun, *More Brilliant Than the Sun: Adventures in Sonic Fiction* (London: Quartet Books, 1998,) 01[012].
[20] Hana Worthen, "For a Skeptical Dramaturgy," *Theatre Topics* 24, no. 3 (2014): 175.

theatre and performance relate to social reality beyond theatre" is help-
ful here.[21]

Second, percussive, *percussivity*, and percussiveness is a concept I sample from hip hop Feminist Brittney Cooper and the members of the Crunk
Feminist Collective's (CFC) term "percussive feminism." The CFC's mission statement explains that percussive—"the sound, vibration or shock
caused by striking together two bodies"—describes the "productive dissonance that occurs as we work at the edge of disciplines, on the margins
of social life, and in the vexed spaces between academic and non-academic
communities." The term as a concept metaphor, assists the members of
the collective as they work to, "divorce [themselves] from 'correct' hegemonic ways of being in favor of following the rhythm of [their] own
heartbeat."[22] Percussivity is not opposed to the harmonious, but it
embraces the power of *bringing the noise* and the importance of *disturbing
the peace* when (or by any means) necessary.[23]

Percussive dramaturgy is a tool, tactic, and tendency of creative and
critical engagement that can track the ways dramatists, specifically those
working through the aesthetics and ethos of hip hop, employ percussivity
to create productive dissonance both artistically and politically in their
plays. Hip hop and hip hop Theatre are spaces where knowledge is con-
stantly created, contested, and recreated. As Daniel Banks points out, hip
hop dramatists find approaches that are contradictory, polyrhythmic, non-
linear, polyvocal, and multilayered in their work.[24] Percussive dramaturgy
as a method of creation and lens of interpretation labors with(in) the contradictory spaces, those shadowy interstices, inhabited by those things sacrificed for narrative and political coherency. To put it differently, it is a

---

[21] Worthen, "For a Skeptical Dramaturgy," 176.

[22] "Mission Statement," *The Crunk Feminist Collective*, accessed December 11, 2020.
http://www.crunkfeministcollective.com/about/

[23] In using Public Enemy's hip hop political anthem "Bringing the noise" (1987) as a
sample, I also want to evoke two other sources: (1) Tricia Rose's *Black Noise* (1994) and (2)
Saidiya Hartman and Stephen Best's use of the phrase black noise in "Fugitive Justice,"
Representations 92, no 1 (2005): 1–15. There, Hartman and Best explain that, "Black noise
represents the kinds of political aspirations that are inaudible and illegible within the prevailing formulas of political rationality; these yearnings are illegible because they are so wildly
utopian and derelict to capitalism (e.g., 'forty acres and a mule,' the end of commodity
production and restoration of the commons, the realization of 'the sublime ideal of freedom,' the resuscitation of the socially dead)" (Best and Hartman 2005, 9).

[24] Daniel Banks, ed. *Say Word! Voices from Hip Hop Theater, an anthology* (Ann Arbor: The
University of Michigan Press, 2014), 11.

dramaturgical practice that "fucks with the gray"[25] areas—as Joan Morgan has identified—between the "rationalized political and aesthetic consensus"[26] and the *ill-logics* of hip hop (see Eshun's epigraph above) in order to amplify the sonic epistemological and ontological whispers of black expressivity in *and against*—as Fred Moten might have it—the (antiblack) World.[27]

Riff/Rupture 2: The (Critical) Love Below, Digging for Bones[28]

Jeff Chang's 2007 book *Total Chaos: The Art and Aesthetic of Hip-Hop* concludes with Danny Hoch's manifesto: "Towards a Hip-Hop Aesthetic."[29] A text that rather than "thinking in disorder"[30]—as the expression "total chaos" might suggest—offers a series of concrete, if not overly confident, assertions about hip hop, its aesthetics, and the conditions that brought it into existence. *Total Chaos* may very well be a "trail book to our [hip hop] universe" (xiii), as Chang suggests; however, its closing piece functions more like a stern enforcement of the rules of the road, on one level, and on another level, a crude roadmap for hip hop

---

[25] Morgan's notion of "grays" refers, mainly, to the ability to critique hip hop with a type of critical celebration which allows for gray areas and nuances to be accounted for. Her term stems from her producing work at the complex intersections of being a black woman, hip hop critic, and devout fan and participant in hip hop culture. See Joan Morgan, *When Chickenheads Come Home to Roost: A Hip-Hop Feminist Breaks it Down* (New York: Simon & Schuster, 2000), 58.

[26] Worthen, "For a Skeptical Dramaturgy," 175.

[27] Moten, Fred. "Hesitant Sociology: Blackness in Poetry."

[28] See the rap duo Outkast's double album *Speakerboxxx/The Love Below* (2003). The first part of this riff's title samples from Andre Ben's album which for me is the B-side to Big Boi's *Spearkerboxxx* and/or vise-a-vera. The second part of the title works to evoke playwright Suzan-Lori Parks's assertion in *The America Play and Other Works* (New York: Theatre Communications Group, 1995) that, "Since history is a recorded or remembered event, theater, for me, is the perfect place to 'make' history—that is, because so much of African-American history has been unrecorded, dismembered, washed out, one of my tasks as playwright is to—through literature and the special strange relationship between theater and real-life—locate the ancestral burial ground, dig for bones, find bones, hear the bones sing, write it down" (Parks 1995, 4).

[29] Danny Hoch, "Toward a hip-hop aesthetic: A manifesto for the hip-hop arts movement." In *Total chaos: The art and aesthetics of hip-hop*, ed., Jeff Chang (New York: Civitas Books, 2006), 349–364.

[30] I borrow the phrase and methodological approach of "thinking in disorder" from RA Judy's book *Sentient Flesh: Thinking in Disorder, Poiesis in Black* (Durham: Duke University Press, 2020).

theater. Hoch's roadmap charts some possible directions, but it is not the territory. That is to say, some of his beliefs and assumptions are not the socio-historical reality.[31] The goal here, then, is to locate a different set of coordinates which might throw into sharp relief the absent presence of what Hoch's map cannot hold or contain, as well as to probe the topo-graphical shadows for alternative subterranean routes which his map(ping) must forget (in order) to remember.

In "Towards A Hip-Hop Aesthetic: A Manifesto for the Hip-Hop Arts Movement," Hoch—one of the founders and artistic directors of the NYC Hip-Hop Theater Festival—outlines the functions, aesthetic elements, power, and importance of hip hop theater. Early in his manifesto, Hoch seems preoccupied with making sure his readers understand that "hip-hop *is* art."[32] This anxiety to "correct" hip hop's misrecognition as something other than "art" causes Hoch to leave unquestioned his own assumption of what art is. Where do assumptions about art come from? Why must hip hop be perceived as art? Why does this perception matter? Matter to whom? What is the difference between an artform and an *artforce*? And, would this affirmed designation of hip hop as art automatically protect the newly deemed "artists" from systemic oppression and structural violence? All of these are questions that elude Hoch's manifesto, but there is some-thing even more significant that escapes his grasp.

Though Hoch carefully examines each of hip hop's four "original" ele-ments (graffiti writing, DJing, emceeing, and breakdancing), he curiously leaves the fifth element un(der)thought. In fact, it is his prudent attention to the other elements that makes his omission of fifth element (knowl-edge) so striking. Afrika Bambaataa describes the fifth element as knowl-edge and *overstanding*, and asserts that it is the element that ties the other four elements together.[33] Since overstanding as Bambaataa declares unites

---

[31] I think it is important to note that a map achieves its coherence as much by what it leaves out as it includes. In this sense, it is much like History, in that it must forget more than it remembers. I am suggesting here that Hoch's approach leaves a great deal *unthought*, as well as leaves much to be desired.

[32] Hoch, "Toward a hip-hop aesthetic," 349. This obsession seems even more out of place when we consider the fact that the manifesto was written in 2006, and not 1986. If there are questions pertaining to hip hop's artistry, perhaps it is not about the genre but the antiblack sentiments targeted at the people associated with it.

[33] "Afrika Bambaataa on growth of galactic Hip-Hop, the 5th Element & the abandon-ment of true Hip-Hop." Feb. 28, 2013, https://www.youtube.com/watch?v=S_fysqsbX8M

and informs all the other elements, it is curious that Hoch wouldn't acknowledge this in his manifesto. How might we work to overstand this indifference to the ways hip hop creates and contests knowledge? I want to suggest that overstanding is a critical stance over and against (one's own) knowledge, a process of knowing that questions how and why one has come to know what they know. Overstanding is skeptical speculation that when applied to the knowledge held and disseminated in Hoch's manifesto would require an interrogation of the assumptions that undergird Hoch's project and projections.

In an article titled "Theory in Black," Lewis Gordon asserts that "theory in black...is theory in jeopardy...it is the dark side of theory, which, in the end, is none other than theory itself, understood as self-reflective, outside itself."[34] Occupying the dark side of theory or the B-side of liberal common sense is the speculative subterranean aims of the fifth element. Taking into consideration the centrality of the fifth element—its jeopardizing self-reflectivity—any analysis of hip hop that does not consider the elements of knowledge and overstanding is surely inadequate. Hoch's detailed evaluation of the performative, stylistic, and aesthetic qualities of hip hop fail to account for the ways in which hip hop creates and contests (orders of) knowledge. Hoch's *under*standing must then be subjected to hip hop's *over*standing in order to reveal the "dark side of [his] theory," as well as uncover "the questions that have been hidden by the [coherency of his] answers?"[35]

Residing in the B-side of Hoch's manifesto, is the issue of hip hop's blackness. Blackness continues to be one of the questions that Hoch attempts to veil by way of his definitive answers. Even though he attempts to avoid, expunge, or "transcend" these questions, they haunt the text. Toward the end of the manifesto, Hoch's attempts to define what constitutes hip hop Theater. He explains that for a dramatic work to be a piece of hip hop Theater it "must fit into the realm of a theatrical performance, and it must be *by*, *about* and *for* the hip-hop generation, participants in hip-hop culture, or both."[36] Hoch's use of the phrase "by, about and for" is curious for two reasons: First, in a leaflet from the Krigwa Players Little

[34] Lewis R. Gordon, "Theory in Black: Teleological Suspensions in Philosophy of Culture." *Qui Parle* 18, no. 2 (2010): 198.
[35] A quote by James Baldwin reads: "The purpose of art is to lay bare the questions hidden by the answers." I have not been able to locate the original source of this quote.
[36] Hoch, "Toward a hip-hop aesthetic," 356.

Negro Theatre (1926) in which W.E.B. Du Bois was the Chairman, one finds the statement: "The plays of the real Negro theatre must be: *About us … By us … For us …* and *Near us.*"[37] Of course, sampling is a part of hip hop aesthetics, but so too is the act of citing in order to extend lyrical, intellectual, and political traditions. The second reason his uncited reference is odd is that Hoch hijacks the first three criteria (about, by, for) but omits the fourth criterion (near). The obvious reason is that Hoch's hip hop community is so vast and all-encompassing that it would be impossible to pinpoint a location where his generational "we" could reside. On the other hand, the more abstract concepts of being *about*, being *by* and being *for* still serve his purpose of conflating the Negro Theatre's racially specific criteria with his own construction of hip hop theater which he imagines as, paradoxically, non-racialized yet multiracial. In the end, The Krigwa Players must go unnamed so that Hoch can "elevate" hip hop from the particular (which he views as limiting) to the mythic-universal which is only accomplished by reimagining hip hop as an "art" that is about, by, and for a nonspecific collection of people that exist everywhere.[38] One might ask what, then, are the unifying "dilemmas of [this] hip-hop generation" that he speaks of?[39]

In pursuit of his universalizing conquest, Hoch asserts that "the notion that hip-hop is solely an African American art form is erroneous." This becomes apparent, Hoch argues, "when we really examine [Hip-Hop's] aesthetics." Where August Wilson might assert that "all art is political," hip hop aesthetics, for Hoch, must be dissociated from "radical political thought" in order to appreciate hip hop as art. Hoch states:

> Unfortunately Hip-hop, bad or good, is almost always relegated to a marginalized

---

[37] "Krigwa Players Little Negro Theatre," https://credo.library.umass.edu/view/page-turn/mums312-b034-i165/#page/4/mode/1up.

[38] I want to punch-phrase the simultaneous evocation and erasure that takes place in Hoch's unreferenced sample. In this gesture, Hoch is able to take the creative and political aspirations of the Krigwa Players and bolster his own project. Du Bois—as well as the other members of the theater: Zora Neale Hurston, Margaret C. Welmon, Eulalie Spence, Louise Reba Latimer, Estelle Anderson, Philitus Joyce, Ernestine Rose, Minnie Brown, to name a few—slip into the "interstitial," as Hortense Spillers has theorized in *Black, White, and in Color: Essays on American Literature and Culture* (Chicago: The University of Chicago Press, 2003), marked by "those punctualities (in a linked sequence of events) that go unmarked so that the mythic view remains undisturbed" (Spillers 2003, 14).

[39] Hoch, "Toward a hip-hop aesthetic," 358.

gray area, a penalty box, if you will, where it is denied the status of art;
it is seen
either as radical political thought, a really bad manifestation of pop culture, or,
with some luck, as novelty entertainment.[40]

Whatever Hoch's notion of art is, it is somehow incompatible with
radical approaches to thinking. One cannot help but hear the absent quali-
fier "black" lurking beneath his use of the phrase "radical political
thought."

Blackness appears again as an absence, when Hoch lays out the "traditions, conditions, and phenomena" that shaped hip hop and its aesthetics:

• An African and Caribbean continuum of storytelling and art
• A polycultural community of both immigrants and migrants
• Appropriation of European cultural traditions and Japanese
  technology
• A legacy of political and gang organizing
• The bumpy transition from post–civil rights and militarized national-
  ist organizing to the supply-side economics of the 1980s
• The devastating effects of Reaganomics on urban America
• The age of accelerated technology.[41]

Again, the descriptive term "black" does not appear in Hoch's account
of the traditions, nor the conditions, nor the phenomena of hip hop's
"origin." Black positionality has no place here. Hoch connects hip hop to
"an African and Caribbean continuum" but elides the violence of the
Middle Passage that marks it. He, then, references "immigrants and
migrants," terms which cannot describe the wayward lives and deaths of
black captives. As for the structures of antagonism targeted at black populations, Hoch veils them with the innocuous phrase, a "bumpy transition,"
rather than the comprehensive murdering of black political leaders.

Admittedly, Hoch's reference to Reaganomics is appropriate; however,
it lacks the explanatory footing to track America's war on Black revolutionary movements and the relentless attacks on black populations under
the guise of the "War on Drugs," which did not solely affect "urban

---

[40] Hoch, "Toward a hip-hop aesthetic," 350.
[41] Hoch, "Toward a hip-hop aesthetic," 350.

America." Hoch is accurate in asserting that the socio-historical conditions of hip hop's birth are complicated because "*we* are still living through
many of the same conditions."[42] However, a much more astute description of these conditions is offered by P. Khalil Saucier and Tryon Woods
when they state that, "hip hop marks the *afterlives* of COINTELPRO,
lynching, the plantation, and the slave trade."[43] Hip hop repositioned
within these traditions, conditions, and phenomena, renders Hoch's use
of the pronoun "we" erroneous at best. If white society takes everything
but the burden from black culture, as Greg Tate suggests, is this an attempt
on Hoch's part to, as a white man, take on these burdens? Does Hoch
believe that being part of the "hip hop community" automatically reposi-
tions him as black in an antiblack World? Or is this the turning gears of
coalition building, lubricated by an ever-expanding and inclusive notion of
the "hip hop community"? Here, hip hop as "community" and "coalition" suffers from a similar problematic that Jared Sexton points out when
he states, "coalitions tend systematically to render supposed common
interests as the concealed particular interests of the most powerful and
privileged elements of the alliance."[44] Is Hoch's desire to be included in
the "community" more important than the interests and demands of the
community?

From within the wake of slavery's afterlife—the "skewed life chances,
limited access to health and education, premature death, incarceration,
and impoverishment"[45]—what similarities and "common interests" bind
Hoch's whiteness to the "melaninated voices that sing [hip hop's] song …
[and] the dark bodies that dance its rhythms"?[46] Can you bind what don't
cling? Could the problematic of Hoch's "we" be located in the difference
and distance between "subjective and objective vertigo,"[47] between a

---

[42] Hoch, "Toward a hip-hop aesthetic," 350. Emphasis added.

[43] Saucier and Woods, "Against Hip Hop Studies," 167.

[44] Jared Sexton, "Afro-Pessimism: The Unclear Word," *Rhizomes: Cultural Studies in Emerging Knowledge*, Issue 29 (2016): n.p.

[45] Saidiya Hartman, *Lose Your Mother: A Journey Along the Atlantic Slave Route* (New York: Farrar, Straus and Giroux, 2007), 6.

[46] Sampled from Tommy Curry "Foreword: Starting from the Bottom," in *Philosophy and Hip-Hip: Ruminations on Postmodern Cultural Form*, ed. Julius Bailey, (New York: Palgrave Macmillan, 2014), iv.

[47] See Frank Wilderson III, "The Vengeance of Vertigo: Aphasia and Abjection in the Political Trials of Black Insurgents" *InTensions* 5.0 (2011), n.p. "Subjective vertigo is vertigo of the event. But the sensation that one is not simply spinning in an otherwise stable environment, that one's environment is perpetually unhinged stems from a relationship to violence

"hope" and "wish,"[48] between contingent and gratuitous violence, between the deck and the hold, or what Jay-Z might call the difference/ distance between recording and recalling?[49] Can Hoch's inclusionary logic hold and contain such profound alterity and can it span such a vast gap or *tear* (as Dionne Brand might have it)?[50] Or must such inclusionary gestures be "displaced by another more radical approach: an ethics of the real, a politics of the imperative, engaged in its interminably downward movement"?[51] To the last question, I answer yes. This, after all, has been the aim of this Riff & Rupture, to get down to the Roots, listen for the echoes of Black Thought, and engage in the imperative task of applying pressure until Things Fall Apart.

Repetition and Revision: Generativity of Black Percussive Noise

Percussive dramaturgy isn't for or against liberal harmony, but it recognizes and deploys the generativity of things being banged together. It is in these collisions, at the anxiety-provoking close edges, those vexed spaces at the margins of social life where new meanings and ways of meaning-making can be created. The goal of percussive dramaturgy, then, is to fall into groove with the rhymes and reasons of a hip hop play, as well as what hip hop puts *into* play and trace the ways it samples, cites and rewrites, punch phrases, and disses not solely as practice (conventions and aesthetics) but as praxis (embodied theory). It is a dramaturgical approach which is both an "analysis and reenactment of rhythm," as Fred Moten might say.[52] It is a practice that doesn't make perfect, that walks, chews gum, and talks shit all at the same time. It is analytical turntablism, courageous enough to contemplate from within, what Joy James has termed, the *dead zone of conceptualization* by speaking black genocide and black achieve-

that cannot be analogized. This is called objective vertigo, a life constituted by disorientation rather than a life interrupted by disorientation. This is structural as opposed to performative violence. Black subjectivity is a crossroads where vertigoes meet, the intersection of performative and structural violence."

[48] Sexton, "Afro-Pessimism: The Unclear Word," para. 35.

[49] "Ain't just rapping for the platinum, y'all record. I recall, 'cause I really been there before," (Jay-Z, "Moment of Clarity").

[50] Dionne Brand, *A Map to the Door of No Return: Notes to Belonging* (Toronto: Vintage Canada 2001), 2.

[51] Sexton, "Afro-Pessimism: The Unclear Word," para 6.

[52] Moten, "Hesitant Sociology: Blackness in Poetry."

ment in the same breath while imagining spaces where we can breathe.[53] At its best, percussive dramaturgy is as concerned with locating answers as it is with discovering better questions, for example, what if the goal is not solely to appear or to represent (black), but to engage in the "incredible inventiveness" of black culture and its "imperative task of transformation" (Wynter 1979)? What if the record is the World?

If the *call* is for a dramaturgy in black—which aims to imagine (as well as interrogate the aesthetics of imagining) what it would mean to take the World apart and [if there is anything salvageable] put it back together—Rickerby Hinds's hip hop dramaturgy offers something of a *response*.

CUT 2: DANCING WITH GHOSTS: BLACK DEATH AND HAUNTING IN RICKERBY HINDS'S *DREAMSCAPE*

Rickerby Hinds's play *Dreamscape* opens with chalk outlines of bodies, materializing onto the stage. The outlines re/present the fatal outcome of Myeisha Mills's (the play's protagonist) violent encounter(s) with officers of the Riverside, California police force. As symbolic objects, however, the chalk outlines gesture toward both the absent presence of her body and the violence it/she suffered. Chalk outlines are rich in symbolic function. They locate and remember the position of a body in its absence, while connecting the violent event to the violated and missing body/corpse. Chalk outlines turn absence into object and object into evidence to make meaning out of the events that unfolded within the crime's *mise-en-scène*.

What is provocative about Hinds's use of the chalk outlines is: on one hand, he employs several outlines to reference or re/member one body. And, on the other hand, he allows the chalk outline to remain on stage throughout the entirety of the play. The outlines are not temporary symbols marking a violent event in the past. In *Dreamscape* the outlines linger as (if) part of the set, World, and paradigm. In other words, the sign(s) of her dying endure in a way that renders her death a "non-event"[54] or a

---

[53] Joy James, "The Dead Zone: Stumbling at the Crossroads of Party Politics, Genocide, and Postracial Racism," *South Atlantic Quarterly* 108, no. 3 (2009): 460–63.

[54] Hartman in "The Dead Book Revisited," *History of the Present* 6, no. 2 (2016) describes the non-event of black death as the "inevitable and wanton violence that routinely produces corpses and denies these deaths any standing as murder. Rather, such deaths constitute the meaning of law and order" (Hartman 2016, 209).

"paradoxical event" as Jaye Austin Williams has theorized.[55] Viewed in this way, Myeisha's death is paradoxical because, though one may be able to trace (like a chalk outline) the beginning, the ending is speculative and uncertain. What is the relationship between the haunting enigmatic event(s) evoked by the outlines and the violence that the play attempts to re/present and reconcile in its dramaturgy? *Dreamscape*, after all, is based on the real-*life* event of the shooting *death* of nineteen-year-old African American Tyisha Miller in Riverside, California.

In this cut, I use the symbol of the chalk outline as an opening, perhaps, a doorway,[56] to explore the ways in which the play *Dreamscape* tarries with/in the space-time of death in order to meditate on the *spooky* relationship between black bodies and structures of violence. First, I track the ways in which Rickerby Hinds (as a hip hop dramatist) abandons the confines of Western realism: a form that would foreclose on the possibility of witnessing black suffering due to its reliance on narrative redemption.[57] Second, I argue that what makes Hinds's meditation possible is his employment of percussive dramaturgy as way to keep in step with what the script terms Myeisha's "life-death-dance." I suggest that the life-death-dance is the performative manifestation of a body being re/collected through ongoing encounters with violence. The recurring and gratuitous nature of this type of violence renders such a death illegible and illogical, existing outside of the space-time of the living. In other words, Hinds's radical use of hip hop aesthetics works to provide a possible space, or an aesthetic (e) scape, for mourning black death, re/membering black bodies, and remixing fragments of black suffering into "evidence."

Teleological Suspension of Dramatic Structure

To commence with(in) death is a *spooky* place to begin. What type of *status quo* does death make? What type of story can a dead body tell? The audience might be led to believe it has arrived too late. Is this the end? Is the

---

[55] Jaye Austin Williams, "Radical Black Drama-as-Theory: The Black Feminist Dramatic on theProtracted Event-Horizon," *Theory & Event* 21, no. 1 (2018): 194.

[56] I am thinking of Trinidadian poet and novelist Dionne Brand's notion of the door of no return as an absent presence, as well as her assertion that, "the door is a place, real, imaginary and imagined," and "it is a door that makes the word *door* impossible and dangerous, cunning and disagreeable" (Brand, *A Map to the Door of No Return: Notes on Belonging*, section 3).

[57] In short, I am thinking here of a narrative based on personal redemption in which a character suffers a series of legible and coherent adversities, overcomes them, and is transformed for the better in the end.

story over? To open with, or begin in, death one must expect a different type of tale, a different type of telling, perhaps, a different type of witnessing. One must anticipate a haunting.

The potency of Hinds's deadly beginning lies in the fact that he does not use death as, simply, an engaging exposition. That is, he doesn't start with Myeisha's death and then flashback to her "life," a plenitude before her fatal encounter with the four Riverside police officers. Instead, Hinds's dramaturgy forces the play to take place (that is: begin and remain) in the time of death. By time of death, I mean two things: first, literally within the interval between the first bullet that pierced the skin of Myeisha's right arm and the last bullet (the twelfth one) that ripped through the right side of her back, piercing her lung. And second, I mean it figuratively and also conceptually, as in death *as* time, a time grasping for, yet resistant to meaning—what scholar and poet David Marriott might refer to as, "dead time"—a time that "never arrives and does not stop arriving, as though by arriving it never happened until it happens again, then it never happened."[58] Hinds's recalibration of temporality invites us to be *spooked*[59] by that which cannot be fully remembered; he challenges us to follow the ghost, and encourages us to listen to (and for) the dead. "The way of the ghost," Avery Gordon reminds us, "is haunting, and *haunting is a very particular way of knowing* what has happened or is happening."[60] To think black suffering with(in) Hinds's *Dreamscape*, it is necessary to follow not only how the play progresses but how it lingers and how such lingering with what remains produces its own knowledge and overstanding.

A sample of stage directions from *Dreamscape* illustrates Hinds's haunting circular use (or abuse) of time, as well as his suspension of traditional narrative progression as an alternative way of witnessing, re/membering, and knowing:

(Prologue) Otis Redding's "White Christmas" gently disquiets the darkness. Lights rise to reveal MYEISHA rising from an autopsy table/DJ setup.

---

[58] David Marriott, *Haunted Life: Visual Culture and Black Modernity* (New Brunswick: RutgersUniversity Press, 2007), xxi.

[59] My use of the term "spook" here is informed by David Marriott's thinking in his book *Haunted Life*. Marriott explains that "the word *spook* reveals a connection between race and terror, magic and surveillance, idolatry and power" (Marriott 2007, 1).

[60] Avery Gordon, *Ghostly Matters: Haunting and the Sociological Imagination* (Minneapolis University of Minnesota Press, 2008), 8. Emphasis added.

She dances the "Twelve Mortal Moves" as the music is spasmodically disrupted by twelve distortions—these are gun shots—each one finds its target in MYEISHA'S body, transforming her movement into a dazzling life-death-dance. She lands in the front seat of her aunt's Nissan Sentra, closes her eyes for a moment then awakens with a jolt.[61]

Note that the character of Myeisha rises from the autopsy table, performs the twelve wounds that cause her death, and then falls into the seat of her aunt's Nissan. This is the vehicle that she will later be shot in, or has already been shot in, since the play opens with her already dead. In the play's conclusion, the stage directions indicate that: *"MYEISHA stops breathing. The CORONER wins the battle, "celebrates" by mixing the following while MYEISHA dances the 12 mortal moves to Otis Redding's 'White Christmas.'"*[62] Moments later, after the Coroner reads off a list of her organs and their respective weights, the stage directions state: *"MYEISHA finishes her dance then quickly climbs into bed—the autopsy table—"she goes to sleep."* The play opens and attempts to close in a ghostly return to the body, to the crime(s) that re/members *her* body, rather than in narrative equilibrium (life), which will later be interrupted by a dramatic event (death). In terms of dramatic structure, Myeisha's dramatic question is answered before it is asked. After all, her battle for life is neither with the officers who killed her nor with EMTs attempting to revive her. Rather, she battles the Coroner whose job it is to determine the cause of death not sustain life. The violence she encounters is both the call and the response; she has arrived too late or, perhaps, too early. Either way when she does appear, her appearance is overdetermined by a looming and inevitable haunted horizon, an ill-fated fatal future.

If Myeisha's future is predetermined, perhaps the radical move is not to progress the narrative but to pause, hold on, remain (in the hold).[63] By tarrying with(in) the space-time of death, its peculiar circularity, Hinds's dramaturgy meditates on the difficulty of adding narrative coherence to a death perceived and positioned as "expected, anticipated, imposed and inescapable."[64] Hinds draws attention to the ways in which structural forces inflict violence on and toward black bodies in ways that resist temporal logic on and off the stage. The nature of this violence (gratuitous

---

[61] Banks, *Say Word! Voices from Hip Hop Theater,* 57.
[62] Banks, *Say Word! Voices from Hip Hop Theater,* 91.
[63] As Frank B. Wilderson III might have it.
[64] Hartman, "The Dead Book Revisited," 209.

and repetitive) unhinges narrative coherence and troubles the logic of cause and effect, which is the engine of Aristotelian dramatic structure.[65] Rather than force the Tyisha Miller's shooting into the confines of causal linearity, Hinds encourages the audience to listen closely to the ghostly whispers, to think on and with the dead, even if it is an affront to the grammar of narrative and dramatic structure.

Some critics have argued that Hinds's use of abstraction might lose focus of, or even "prettify," the real violence surrounding Miller's shooting.[66] Though I am sensitive to the problematics that such criticisms seek to address, I feel that they misinterpret the reasons why Hinds might opt to depict violence at this level of abstraction. Hinds, I suggest, is thinking of Miller's death at the intersection of race and violence. Hortense Spillers reminds us that "race: haunts the air where women and men in social organization are most reasonable."[67] Hinds's use of abstraction challenges the notion of reason and rationale that traditional dramatic structure might impose on the narrative. Western dramatic realism would fail to comprehend (or represent) such a comprehensive violence as the type that haunts Miller's death (and life). Hinds, then, when confronted with the *unreasonable reasons*[68] of racialized violence seeks out alternative registers for storying: perhaps something akin to Myeisha's plea at the end of the play, namely, to "turn [her] story into a dream fable."[69] The questions become: what evades the structure of dramatic realism that might be apprehended through a type of dream "logic"? And, what can be learned from the percussive and contradiction-embracing nature of a dream?

In dreams, the logic of cause and effect is often distorted, and Hinds works to suspend traditional structure and form, by employing this peculiar "logic." Poet and novelist Dionne Brand explains that, "One is not in

---

[65] I am thinking with and alongside of some of Frank B. Wilderson III's arguments in his article "Close-Up: Fugitivity and the Filmic Imagination: Social Death and Narrative Aporia in *12 Years a Slave*," *Black Camera, An International Film Journal 7*, no. 1 (2015): 134–149.

[66] See Ed Rampell's "Screamscape: The timely play "Dreamscape" about police killings," *People's World*. Peoplesworld.org, April 20, 2015.

[67] Spillers, *Black, White, and in Color*, 379.

[68] I am riffing with Lewis Gordon's ruminations on a quote from Frantz Fanon in his article "Reasoning in Black: Africana Philosophy Under the Weight of Misguided Reason," in a *I Am Because We Are: Readings in Africana Philosophy*, edited by Fred Hord and Jonathan Lee, 281–293. (Amherst: University of Massachusetts Press, 2016). There, Gordon writes: "Yet Fanon's response to unreasonable reason was not to *force* reason to become reasonable, which would be *unreasonable*" (italics in original; Gordon 2016, 290).

[69] Banks, *Say Word! Voices from Hip Hop Theater*, 87.

control in dreams; dreams take place, the dreamer is captive, even though it is the dreamer who is dreaming."[70] Brand's notion of the imprisoning nature of dreams is echoed by the opening lines of *Dreamscape* where Myeisha asks: "Ever have one of those dreams/where nothing comes out when you [try to] scream?"[71] Myeisha's question serves as a type of refrain throughout the play, a haunting reminder that she is held captive in a dream, the dream of her own death, unable to scream or articulate her frightening position. "First I can't holla/Now I can't move...Feel like a prisoner of war and I can't even move," Myeisha explains at one point in the play.

To re/remember Myeisha's (and by extension Tyisha Miller's) story, to recover her body, to mourn her death, Hinds disses (as in disrespects but also disarticulates) Western dramatic structure and works to meditate on the "unthought position"[72] of blackness in general, and black death in particular. If the black body, as Frank Wilderson III argues, "magnetizes bullets,"[73] as it appears Tyisha Miller's did, how does one narrativize a body that is simultaneously the cause and effect of violence? How does one characterize a body that/who, even when unconscious, manifests twelve gunshot wounds? Rather than forcing Myeisha's story (read: her death) into narrative or temporal logic, and thereby eclipsing the "untimeliness" of her death,[74] Hinds forsakes the legibility of dramatic linearity for the obscurity of a dream-like atemporality in order to consider the "deathliness"[75] that haunts her story, her body, as well as the body of evidence surrounding the case. By doing so, *Dreamscape* conjures the *spectral moments*[76] of black death, which are unable to be fully incorporated into the grammar of woken life. After all, dreams are where one wrestles with their unconscious, with the unthinkable, and with the *unthought*.

[70] Brand, *A Map to the Door of No Return*, section 10.
[71] Banks, *Say Word! Voices from Hip Hop Theater*, 55.
[72] See Saidiya V. Hartman and Frank B. Wilderson, "The Position of the Unthought" *Qui Parle* 13, no. 2 (2003): 183–201.
[73] Wilderson III, *Red, White & Black*, 83.
[74] John Murillo III, "Quantum Blackanics: Untimely Blackness, and Black Literature Out of Nowhere," PhD diss. (Brown University, 2016), 4.
[75] Marriott, *Haunted Life* 231.
[76] A "spectral moment," Derrida explains is "a moment that no longer belongs to time," (Derrida 1994, xx).

Hinds and Hip Hop Aesthetic

Hinds's use of layering, sampling, and remixing—all central components of hip hop—are what assist him in his working beyond traditional narrative structure and into the realm of dream "logic." Here, I will isolate three key elements of Hinds's use of hip hop aesthetics (minimalism, sampling, and layering) and discuss how they influence and inform his percussive dramaturgy.

All I need is one mic
—Nas[77]

Everybody's a rapper, but few flow fatalIt's fucked up, it all started from two turntables
—Nas[78]

Among many things, hip hop is, largely, a minimalist art form. With two turntables, a mixer, and a crate full of records, a DJ can rock a party for hours on end. The original Rap group arrangement was (and often still is) a DJ and an Emcee. As a hip hop dramatist, Hinds utilizes this minimalist aesthetic in the play by using only two characters: Myeisha Mills and The DJ. The character of Myeisha speaks in a manner which moves fluidly from rap to spoken word poetry. She serves as a type of emcee, the one who will provide the lyrics or story for the evening, while The DJ will sample through a constellation of sonic texts to create the soundscape. In the play, however, Hinds's DJ serves another important function. By playing a host of other characters, The DJ serves as a trickster figure, or a conjurer. In a sense, The DJ not only samples outside texts (such as officer testimony and an autopsy report), s/he becomes them through a type of performative manifestation. As the stage directions explain, *"All other characters in the play should manifest themselves through the DJ."*[79] Rather than have all the individuals involved in Miller's shooting represented by a character, Hinds employs only a DJ and Emcee. This use of hip hop minimalism adds to the mythical and abstracted style of his dramaturgy. This is not realism and, as Myeisha says in the play, "This ain't gonna be one of them feel-good shows" (Banks 56). Hinds complicates the telling of

[77] Nas. "One Mic." *Stillmatic*, 2001. Columbia.
[78] Nas. "Carry On Tradition." *Hip Hop Is Dead*, 2006. Columbia.
[79] Banks, *Say Word! Voices from Hip Hop Theater*, 55.

Miller's murder by the four Riverside police by having it manifest through only two black actors.[80]

The minimalist approach also supports Hinds's use of hip hop sampling. Sampling, scholar Nicole Hodges Persley explains is, "the practice of identifying and borrowing particular parts of a song and using them to create a new work."[81] Sampling, Persley suggests elsewhere, "can be adopted as a subversive methodological and theoretical tool."[82] Hinds employs the subversive qualities of sampling and layering by placing event and evidence into a percussive encounter, for example, the Coroner/DJ samples from texts surrounding Tyisha Miller's shooting. This textual collision creates generative dissonance and allows Hinds to comment on the events, adding and layering a type of meta-commentary. When Toni (Myeisha's cousin) calls the police, for example, Hinds has the DJ "drop" Public Enemy's "911 Is a Joke." This layered commentary on policing and blackness foreshadows the deadly result that dialing 911 had for Myeisha/Tyisha. Hinds, like The DJ in *Dreamscape*, operates on the tragic event and the discourse that surrounds it by cutting, splicing, and mixing the body of evidence to create new ways of knowing and witnessing.

In the play, evidence, events, and testimonies are not presented separately, but layered on top of each other. Hinds's use of layering holds event(s) and discourse in productive tension with each other. But more importantly, the use of layering challenges the ways the audience might interpret these events. Hip hop has the abilities to work with fragments, function in contradictions, and generate (by use of sampling and layering) new methods and meanings. Hinds's dramaturgy, then, employs what Kodwo Eshun terms the, "onomatopoeic illogic called hip hop," to attempt to mourn and meditate on the violent excess that haunts Miller's death. Through the character of Myeisha and the aesthetics of hip hop, Hinds is able to make visible that which spooks Miller's remains: the excess of violence that precedes and anticipates black life/death in an antiblack World. This is not redemptive closure, but rather a radical call to meditate on black death outside of Aristotelian dramatic structure and beyond the confines of liberal commonsense, to agree to make all tales of black death

---

[80] The two productions I have had the chance to see, as well as the production photos available online use two Black actors, one female and one male.

[81] Nicole Persley, "Sampling," in *Reading Contemporary Performance: Theatricality Across Genres*, eds. Meiling Cheng and Gabrielle H. Cody (New York: Routledge, 2016), 260.

[82] Persley, "Sampling," 260.

"dream fables."[83] The question, then, becomes what is one to re/member from this specific dream fable?

The answer, I argue, lies in the ways Hinds provocatively samples and layers the autopsy report, specifically toward the end of the play. Hinds presents the polices' gunshots and the path of the bullets as a type of ceremonial performance. The DJ, sampling from the autopsy report, creates a narrative of the bullets' journeys from gun barrel to victim's body. While The DJ constructs the story of the bullets, Myeisha reacts to their violent effects by performing a dance named after each bullet's entry location. Notice how Hinds ritualistically re/presents the trajectory of the tenth bullet that strikes Myeisha's body:

(DJ samples a series of "tens." MYEISHA does the "upper left forehead" move.)
CORONER: The entrance to gunshot number ten is located on the left upper forehead.
  right upper arm. This is a typical distant gunshot wound entrance. The course of the
  projectile is through the skin of the forehead, entering the cranium through the left frontal
  bone, through the left and right frontal lobes of the brain, through the right orbit
  perforating and rupturing the right ocular globe and exiting the right orbit. The direction
  of the projectile is back-to-front, left-to-right and downward 45 degrees. This is a fatal
  distant gunshot wound to the head.[84]

The difference between the narrative coherence imbued in the "life" of the bullet lies in stark contrast to the narrative disjointedness of Myeisha's death. The tragic irony is that only the bullets "enjoy" true narrative unity. Myeisha's "narrative," emerges as fragments and is continuously interrupted by the violence of the bullets. It is as if her story exists outside the realm of narration or her narrative attempts arrive too late to re/member her, to render her death intelligible.

In one of the rare moments where Myeisha endeavors to make "sense" of her death or her dying, she does so by thinking it in terms of hip hop. "I bet you ain't seen no female MC who's been shot as many times as me,"

[83] Banks, *Say Word! Voices from Hip Hop Theater,* 87.
[84] Banks, *Say Word! Voices from Hip Hop Theater,* 87.

Myeisha states, and later explains: "It's been a year since they shot Biggie/ Since Tupac was killed it's been two/It just makes sense that this should happen to me now." The stage directions are even more telling:

> *(A red bandana/blood begins to ooze from MYEISHA'S headphones/ear. She stops rapping and tries to push bandana/blood back into her head. When she realizes she can't push it back in, she pulls out the bandana and ties it around her head TUPAC style—she becomes him [...] MYEISAH re-ties the bandana BIGGIE style—she becomes him).*[85]

Hinds's use of the forward slash or virgule suggests a type of metatheatrical gesture that I read as an attempt to connect the theatrical (bandana) with the real (blood). It is as if the representation of death in the play cannot be separated from actual deaths off the stage: Miller, Tupac, Biggie, etc. What is also provocative about the Tupac and Biggie sample is that in order to add legibility to the violence that subsumes Miller's death, Hinds renders it analogous to two other deaths, two deaths which are equally haunted and shrouded in both questions and contradictions. Thought another way, for Myeisha to comprehend her own death she must think it not from a singular subject position but from a space of plurality. She must "become" them.

Through his use of sampling and layering, Hinds raises the level of abstraction from Myeisha's (symbolic) death and Tyisha Miller's (real) death to black people's (social) death in general in order to locate a register in which to address black suffering. If mourning, as Derrida explains, "consists always in attempting to ontologize remains, to make them present, in the first place by *identifying* the bodily remains and by *localizing* the dead," Hinds's dramaturgy works to provide a space for localizing, identifying, re-collecting, and mourning what remains.[86] Even if what remains, cannot fully be re/presented or remembered. In a World where black bodies are symbolically and materially tethered to violent *forces*, meditating on black death, blackness and death, requires that we find ways to access new, possibly unnerving, frequencies, to listen in (and for) the whispers from the shadows, even if what the dead utter, what they request, is too spooky, too unsettling for our (inner) ears.

[85] Banks, *Say Word! Voices from Hip Hop Theater,* 89.
[86] Jacques Derrida, *Specters of Marx: The State of Debt, The Work of Mourning, and The New International.*, trans Peggy Kamuf (London: Routledge, 1994), 9. Emphasis in the original.

BIBLIOGRAPHY

"Afrika Bambaataa on growth of galactic Hip-Hop, the 5th Element & the abandonment of true Hip-Hop." Feb. 28, 2013, https://www.youtube.com/watch?v=S_fysqsbX8M

Afropessimism, an introduction. Racked & Dispatched, 2017.

Banks, Daniel, ed. *Say Word! Voices from Hip Hop Theater, an anthology.* Ann Arbor: The University of Michigan Press, 2014.

Basu, Dipannita, and Sidney J. Lemelle, eds. *The Vinyl Ain't Final: Hip Hop and the Globalization of Black Popular Culture.* Ann Arbor: Pluto Press, 2006.

Best, Stephen and Saidiya Hartman. "Fugitive Justice." *Representations* 92, no 1 (2005): 1-15.

Brand, Dionne. *A Map to the Door of No Return: Notes to Belonging,* Toronto: Vintage Canada 2001.

Big Fun in the Big Town. Bram Van Splunteren. VPRO, 1986

Chang, Jeff. *Total Chaos: The Art and Aesthetics of Hip-Hop.* Civitas Books, 2007.

Curry, Tommy. "Foreword: Starting from the Bottom," In *Philosophy and Hip-Hip: Ruminations on Postmodern Cultural Form,* ed. Julius Bailey, ix-xiv. New York: Palgrave Macmillan, 2014.

Derrida, Jacques. *Of Grammatology.* Baltimore: The Johns Hopkins University Press, 1977.

———. *Specters of Marx: The State of Debt, The Work of Mourning, and The New International.* Trans Peggy Kamuf. London: Routledge, 1994.

Eshun, Kodwo. *More Brilliant Than the Sun: Adventures in Sonic Fiction.* London: Quartet Books, 1998.

Gordon, Avery. *Ghostly Matters: Haunting and the Sociological Imagination.* Minneapolis University of Minnesota Press, 2008.

Gordon, Lewis. "Theory in Black: Teleological Suspensions in Philosophy of Culture." *Qui Parle* 18, no. 2 (2010): 193-214.

———. "Reasoning in Black: Africana Philosophy Under the Weight of Misguided Reason." In a *I Am Because We Are: Readings in Africana Philosophy,* edited by Fred Hord and Jonathan Lee, 281-293. Amherst: University of Massachusetts Press, 2016.

Hartman, Saidiya. *Lose Your Mother: A Journey Along the Atlantic Slave Route.* Farrar, Straus and Giroux, 2007.

———. "Venus in Two Acts." *Small Axe* 12, no. 2 (2008): 1-14.

———. "The Dead Book Revisited." *History of the Present* 6, no. 2 (2016): 208-215

Hartman, Saidiya V., and Frank B. Wilderson. "The Position of the Unthought." *Qui Parle* 13, no. 2 (2003): 183-201.

Hoch, Danny. "Toward a hip-hop aesthetic: A manifesto for the hip-hop arts movement." In *Total chaos: The art and aesthetics of hip-hop,* ed., Jeff Chang (New York: Civitas Books, 2006): 349-364.

Holland, Sharon P. "The Question of Normal." *GLQ: A Journal of Lesbian and Gay Studies* 10, no. 1 (2003): 128-131.

hooks, bell. *Black Looks: Race and Representation*. Boston: South End Press, 1992.

James, Joy. "The Dead Zone: Stumbling at the Crossroads of Party Politics, Genocide, and Postracial Racism." *South Atlantic Quarterly* 108, no. 3 (2009): 460-63.

Judy, R. A. *Sentient Flesh: Thinking in Disorder, Poiesis in Black*. Durham: Duke University Press, 2020.

"Krigwa Players Little Negro Theatre," https://credo.library.umass.edu/view/pageturn/mums312-b034-i165/#page/1/mode/1up

Marriott, David. *Haunted Life: Visual Culture and Black Modernity*. New Brunswick: Rutgers University Press, 2007.

"Mission Statement," The Crunk Feminist Collective, accessed December 11, 2020. http://www.crunkfeministcollective.com/about/

Morgan, Joan. *When Chickenheads Come Home to Roost: A Hip-Hop Feminist Breaks it Down*. New York: Simon & Schuster, 2000.

Moten, Fred. "Hesitant Sociology: Blackness in Poetry." UChicago Division of the Humanities. July 31, 2017. Video, 51:37, https://www.youtube.com/watch?v=jlk4X9tZmt4&t=1965s

Murillo III John, "Quantum Blackanics: Untimely Blackness, and Black Literature Out of Nowhere." PhD diss. Brown University, 2016.

Parks, Suzan-Lori. *The America Play and Other Works*. New York: Theatre Communications Group, 1995.

Persley, Hodges Nicole. "Sampling." In *Reading Contemporary Performance: Theatricality Across Genres*, eds. Meiling Cheng and Gabrielle H. Cody, 260-1. New York: Routledge, 2016.

Rampell, Ed. "Screamscape: The timely play 'Dreamscape' about police killings." *People's World*. Peoplesworld.org, April 20, 2015.

Rose, Tricia. *Black Noise: Rap Music and Black Culture in Contemporary America*. Middletown: Wesleyan University Press, 1994.

Sarup, Madan. *An Introductory Guide to Post-structuralism and Post-modernism*. Longman, 1993.

Saucier, P. Khalil and Tryon Woods. "Hip Hop Studies in Black." *Journal of Popular Music Studies* 26, no 2-3 (2014): 268-294.

Saucier, P. Khalil. "Against Hip Hop Studies." In *On Marronage: Ethical Confrontations with Antiblackness*, eds. P. Khalil Saucier and Tryon P. Woods. (Trenton: Africa World Press, 2015).

Sexton, Jared. *Amalgamation Schemes: Antiblackness and the Critique of Multiracialism*. Minneapolis: University of Minnesota Press, 2008.

———. "The Social Life of Social Death: On Afro-Pessimism and Black Optimism." *InTensions Journal*, issue 5 (2011), ISSN# 1913-5874.

———. "Afro-Pessimism: The Unclear Word." *Rhizomes: Cultural Studies in Emerging Knowledge*, Issue 29 (2016) https://doi.org/10.20415/rhiz/029.e02.

Spillers, Hortense. *Black, White, and in Color: Essays on American Literature and Culture*. Chicago: The University of Chicago Press, 2003.

———. "Mama's Baby, Papa's, Too." *Trans-Scripts* 1 (2011): 1-4, https://www.humanities.uci.edu/collective/hetr/trans-scripts/2011_01_02.pdf.

Tate, Greg, ed. *Everything but the Burden: What White People are Taking from Black Culture*. New York: Broadway Books, 2003.

"What's Radical About 'Mixed Race'? Minelle Mahtani, Ann Morning, & Jared Sexton," Asian/Pacific/American Institute. May 18, 2015, https://www.youtube.com/watch?v=jSMQpRzcGpA

Worthen, Hana. "For a Skeptical Dramaturgy." *Theatre Topics* 24, no. 3 (2014): 175-186.

Wilderson III, Frank B. *Red, White & Black: Cinema and the Structure of U.S. Antagonisms*. Durham: Duke University Press, 2010.

Wilderson III. "The Vengeance of Vertigo: Aphasia and Abjection in the Political Trials of Black Insurgents." *InTensions* 5.0 (2011) http://www.yorku.ca/intent/issue5/articles/frankbwildersoniii.php.

Wilderson III. "The Vengeance of Vertigo: Aphasia. "Close-Up: Fugitivity and the Filmic Imagination: Social Death and Narrative Aporia in *12 Years a Slave*." *Black Camera, An International Film Journal* 7, no. 1 (2015): 134-149.

———. *Afropessimism*. New York: Liveright, 2020.

Williams, Jaye Austin. "Radical Black Drama-as-Theory: The Black Feminist Dramatic on the Protracted Event-Horizon." *Theory & Event* 21, no. 1 (2018): 191-214.

Wynter, Sylvia. "On How We Mistook the Map for the Territory, and Reimprisoned Ourselves in Our Unbearable Wrongness of Being, of *Desêtre*: Black Studies Toward the Human Project," *Not Only the Master's Tools: African American Studies in Theory and Practice*, eds. Lewis Gordon and Jane Anna Gordon, Routledge, 2006.

———. Do Not Call Us Negros: How "Multicultural" Textbooks Perpetuate Racism. San Francisco: Aspire Books, 1990.

Discography

Hill, Lauryn. "Final Hour." Recorded August 1998. Track 7 on The Miseducation of Lauryn Hill. Ruffhouse, compact disc.

Jay-Z, "Moment of Clarity." Recorded July—October 2003. Track 8 on The Black Album. Def Jams, compact disc.

Nas. "One Mic." Recorded 2000. Track 4 on Stillmatic. Ill Will/Columbia, compact disc.

———. "Carry on Tradition." Recorded 2005-2006. Track 3 on Hip Hop is Dead. Def Jam, compact disc.
Outkast. Speakerboxxx/The Love Below. Recorded September 2003. LaFace, compact disc.
Public Enemy. "Bring the Noise." Recorded 1987. Def Jam, compact disc.

On the Dilemma of MAN: Intersections Reconsidered

P. Khalil Saucier and Tryon P. Woods

In early January of 2014, sixteen-year-old Darrin Manning and his high school basketball teammates were on their way to a game when they were chased by Philadelphia police officers for looking suspicious.[1] Manning was tackled to the ground, roughed up, handcuffed, and eventually "frisked" by a female officer. Manning's account of the episode was corroborated by eyewitnesses: "She patted me down again, and then I felt her reach, and she grabbed my butt...And then she grabbed and squeezed

---

[1] Gary Younge, "If Darrin Manning were a high school dropout, he'd still have the right to walk the streets unmolested, *The Guardian*, January 27, 2014. Accessed May 1, 2024. https://www.theguardian.com/commentisfree/2014/jan/27/darrin-manning-high-school-deserving-victims

---

P. K. Saucier
Department of Critical Black Studies, Bucknell University, Lewisburg, PA, USA
e-mail: pks008@bucknell.edu

T. P. Woods (✉)
University of Massachusetts, Dartmouth, Department of Crime & Justice Studies, Dartmouth, MA, USA
e-mail: twoods@umassd.edu

© The Author(s), under exclusive license to Springer Nature Switzerland AG 2025
P. K. Saucier (ed.), *Critical Essays on Hip Hop and the Study of Hip Hop*, https://doi.org/10.1007/978-3-031-80763-3_6

121

again and pulled down. And that's when I heard something pop, like I felt it pop." Manning's story of sexual assault was later dismissed and the officer in question was cleared of all wrongdoing.[2] Despite official pronouncements, even mainstream media accounts appeared to register the mundane nature of Manning's sexual violation. Rather than outrage or even umbrage, one local newspaper's observation, "cop back on the job after squeezing teen's testicles," signaled habituation to what Tommy Curry calls "sexualized police violence" or "police sexual misconduct," but what is in fact the sexual violence essential to policing, nothing more, nothing less.[3]

The historical log of antiblack sexual violence is a long one. Manning's case reflects a deep-seated tradition of slave masters, police, and other whites perpetrating sexual violence against black people with impunity. This is the empirical record of "racism, policing's other name, as an act of sexual violence that produces the punishment of race."[4] In 2016, the City of Milwaukee awarded a $5 million settlement to seventy-four young black men, one as young as fifteen years old, who were subjected to illegal body cavity and strip searches by the Milwaukee Police Department.[5] In 2020, a group of forty black men who were former athletes at the University of Michigan came forward to testify to the pattern of sexual assault across several decades at the hands of the physician for the athletics department.[6] These spectacles obscure the everyday reality of the

---

[2] Larry Miller, "Officer cleared in Darrin Manning Investigation, *The Philadelphia Tribune*, July 17, 2014. Accessed May 1, 2024. https://www.phillytrib.com/news/officer-cleared-in-darrin-manning-investigation/article_7868b987-b3ee-5a6c-a9e5-ee8f6219df91.html

[3] The Associated Press, "Officer accused of rupturing teens testicle during search," *NBC 10*, January 18, 2014. Accessed May 1, 2024. https://www.nbcphiladelphia.com/news/national-international/officer-accused-of-rupturing-teens-testicle-during-search/85663/; Tommy J. Curry, *The Man-Not: Race, Class and Genre and the Dilemmas of Black Manhood* (Philadelphia: Temple University Press, 2017), 142–43; See also, Tryon P. Woods *Blackhood Against the Police Power: Punishment and Disavowal in the "Post-Racial" Era*, (East Lansing: Michigan State University Press, 2019).

[4] Woods, *Blackhood*, xii.

[5] Loevy and Loevy, "Milwaukee Settles Racially Tinged Cavity Strip Search Suit," *Loevy. com*, January 19, 2016. Accessed May 1, 2024. https://www.loevy.com/milwaukee-settles-racially-tinged-body-cavity-strip-search-suit-with-74-black-men/

[6] Eric Chilburn, "Black Men Participating in College Sports May Be More Vulnerable to Sexual Abuse," *Insight Into Higher Ed*, March 16, 2022. Accessed May 1, 2024.https://www.insightintodiversity.com/black-men-participating-in-college-sports-may-be-more-vulnerable-to-sexual-abuse/

unnamed.[7] Antiblack sexual violence is the foreseeable outcome of a process that begins with the racist act of looking ("racial profiling"). The agents of bodily harm from across the legal, medical, and educational professions are occasionally prosecuted for "negligence" with respect to the "flesh" in their custody, but the primary acts of black bodily desire, seizure, and dispossession generate nary a condemnation, let alone prosecution. It is precisely these scopic and possessive acts that drive popular culture representations of race, power, and violence. The "tactile properties of enslavement" remain endlessly pleasurable and profitable.[8]

Nearly two months after the Philadelphia police sexually assaulted Darrin Manning, Fayetteville, North Carolina emcee J. Cole dropped his cinematic music video "GOMD" from his third studio album, 2014's *Forest Hills Drive*.[9] By our estimation, "get off my dick" and the video in which it becomes an exultant guttural refrain for victorious slave rebels, rejects the discourse of black sexual violence and black male pathology. More importantly, however, it also complicates the preferred reading of hip hop as an expression of black self-possession. Hortense Spillers' distinction between the bodies of enslaved Africans and black flesh is apropos here: "The flesh is like the first level of the body ... [and] in order to get to the body, you must go through flesh."[10] The flesh connotes that symbolic order within which the sexual violence severing the black body from the human body disappears inside an endless catalogue of metaphorical and literal mutilations. It is from the flesh that the expression "GOMD" emerges. In other words, it is *not* the utterance of a sovereign individual in possession of an autonomous self and its accordant bodily integrity. J. Cole's subversion of pathological blackness in "GOMD" serves as a necessary bridge between a humanist notion of black self-possession popular among hip hop studies and a conception of black body politics emergent at an earlier juncture in black movement. Instead of reading "GOMD"

---

[7] This case precedes and anticipates the facts of the more well-publicized case of Larry Nassar who assaulted female athletes in his care at Michigan State University and the USA national gymnastics program. In 2017–2018, Nassar was convicted and sentenced to over 175 years in prison for his crimes. The perpetrator of the assaults at the University of Michigan, Robert Anderson, died in 2008 without ever being held accountable, although a mediation case with the University remains ongoing.

[8] Ferreira da Silva, Denise. "Sending Language into Battle: Interview with Hortense J. Spillers." *boundary 2* 51, no. 1 (2024): 22.

[9] "GOMD," J. Cole, *2014 Forest Hills Drive*, Columbia, 2014.

[10] Ferreira da Silva, Denise. "Sending Language into Battle," 22.

as a visual and sonic montage of self-possession, as is the popular tendency within hip hop studies, we see it as a map of slavery's consumptive practices. Cole's song and video unmask racial slavery as a socio-historical process of cultivated aesthetic and existential appreciation that literally whets and slakes the appetite for blackness.

The "MAN" of our title is a double entendre. M-A-N are the initials of Mark Anthony Neal, a leading critic of black masculinity in hip hop. In one sense, we use MAN to signify how hip hop, the industry of academic pronouncements about difference to which it is connected, and the larger practices of consumption to which both are in fee invest in a narrowly biocentric body politic. MAN is deeply critical of what he and others who align themselves with academic black feminism view as hip hop's gender and sexuality problem. At the same time, then, MAN also indicates the ongoing grip of modern humanist thought. Sylvia Wynter refers to this vexation as the problem of the "monohumanism" of "Man": the capacity of Western civilization to both elaborate a universal conception of what it means to be a human being as if it were the only natural and proper form of existence *and* to quarantine all critiques of this construct within humanism's biologically imagined and ethno-class specific mode of being.[11] Neal, academic black feminism, and hip hop studies, together, exemplify this failure to set aside the pleasures of humanist thought. Humanism's central conceit of the possessive individual, its sovereignty over the body, and an imagined developmental trajectory of history prove a particularly difficult set of pleasures for hip hop scholars and critics to set aside and reveal the yearning for success, achievement, and overcoming that underwrites much of hip hop, hip hop studies, and academic black feminism. The dilemma of MAN, therefore, is how to read an ostensibly resistant cultural expression—hip hop—in terms that explicate the nature of the paradigm, rather than as Neal and black feminist hip hop studies scholars do, in ways that reify it by making it more opaque.

In short, our reading of "GOMD" is an occasion to rethink performance, commodification, and consumption not simply as momentary acts, but also as indices of the extant ontological condition of racialization. We read Cole's song and the accompanying video in terms of its epistemic entanglements in excess of the aesthetic. This reading renders visible the power behind MAN. Put differently, this chapter has little to do with hip

[11] See for example Katherine McKittrick, ed. *Sylvia Wynter: On being human as praxis,* (Duke University Press, 2015).

hop per se, nor is it concerned with enjoining MAN's interest in imagining hip hop as a response to the history of slavery.[12] Harriet Jacobs famously observed that "no pen can give adequate description to the all-pervading corruption produced by slavery."[13] Riffing on Jacobs' insight, this chapter suggests, contrary to the claims of MAN, that no poetic lyric or dramatic performance can adequately stand in for the violence produced by antiblackness.

READING GENDER: Perturbing Black Feminism

The esteem accorded black feminism in the twenty-first century multicultural academy and in hip hop studies specifically intersects with the phenomenon of antiblack state violence in an interesting but thorny manner. Despite the growing condemnation of police killings, stop-and-frisk tactics, and racial profiling, scenes of antiblack state violence remain ubiquitous across the multimedia platforms through which people consume their realities. Of course, these are constructed realities shaped through the various fictional and non-fictional images of blackness that circulate within a cultural context in which narratives of black criminality, dangerousness, incorrigibility, and pathology tend to overwhelm notions of black victimization or oppression. It is very difficult to displace the cultural logic of antiblackness which maintains that the black victim of policing, no matter the injustice of the outcome, simply was not behaving the way a human being ought to behave.

Ironically, this narrative intersects with a common refrain in academic black feminism: the toxic heteronormativity of black masculinity, or "hypermasculinity." Informed by the seminal but specious work of Patricia Hill Collins and bell hooks, black feminism aids and abets the mischaracterization of black males as sexual deviants and predators, as lazy, and as dangerous criminals.[14] Hip hop studies extends this construction of a psychopathological black masculinity by focusing on how hip hop culture

---

[12] See for example, Regina N. Bradley, "Re-imagining slavery in the hiP-hoP imagination," *South: a scholarly journal* 49.1 (2016): 3–24.

[13] Jacobs writes in *Incidents in the Life of a Slave Girl*, as quoted in Thomas Foster, "The sexual abuse of Black men under American slavery." *Journal of the History of Sexuality* 20.3 (2011): 453.

[14] See Patricia Hill Collins, *Black Sexual Politics: African Americans, Gender, and the New Racism* (New York: Routledge, 2004); bell hooks, *We Real Cool: Black Men and Masculinity* (New York: Routledge, 2004).

portrays black males as criminals, gangsters, and victimizers of women and queers. As MAN states in his book on "illegible black masculinities," hip hop culture is "largely premised on highly contrived essentialist notions of black masculinity."[15] Neal attempts to counter the popular narrative around "hip-hop thugs and strip-club denizens…" in order to make legible the gender identities and sexualities of black males who do not fit into these stereotypes.[16] This is the specious premise MAN borrows from black feminism: since all stereotypes are patently false, by definition, *no* black males fit into the trope of hypermasculinity. Neal's effort to counter this trope by sketching a black masculinity that does not seek the subordination of women, that identifies as queer, or that imagines agency in nonviolent terms thus accepts the narrative of black gender and sex pathology promulgated by antiblack society and buttressed by academic black feminism as self-evident. Hip hop studies' refutations of this narrative, therefore, recenter the same epistemological order that constructed the liberal humanism of Man. Neal and other hip hop scholars rely upon the humanist conceit of self-possession in which subjects are said to "have" gender, "are" gendered, or "do" gender to imagine black masculinities that transcend the "meta-identities that define most (if not all) people of African descent who live in the United States."[17] The black male feminist relies upon, and thus necessarily reproduces, the brute and the thug—if only to call them out, discredit them, and substitute a less offensive and more complicated figure of blackness in their stead.

For example, in *Looking for Leroy*, Neal attempts to wrest the black male imago from the clutches of white supremacy by queering representations of black masculinity. As Neal plainly states, "I am particularly concerned with the productive value of having the theoretical worlds of black feminist and queer theory…travel through the body of a highly visible and influential masculine icon of hip-hop, as an alternative iteration of diaspora."[18] Neal focuses on the musical career of Jay Z, viewing the rapper as exhibiting a "hip hop cosmopolitanism" that breaks from the

---

[15] Mark Anthony Neal, *Looking for Leroy: Illegible Black Masculinities* (New York: NYU Press, 2013), 63.

[16] Neal, *Looking for Leroy*, 3. On this front, Neal sees what he calls ""queered" visions of urban blackness…" as a counternarrative to heteronormative gender identities and sexualties.

[17] Mark Anthony Neal, "NIGGA: The twenty-first-Century Theoretical Superhero," *Cultural Anthropology* 28.3 (2013): 557–58.

[18] Neal, *Looking for Leroy*, 39.

"closeted identities" that populate mainstream hip hop culture.[19] To *be* cosmopolitan, is to exceed the tropes of thuggery, and in the end, to be what Neal calls a "legitimate citizen of the world."[20] Cosmopolitanism, therefore, is categorical evidence of a radical becoming that breaks from the black male imago. Thugs, hustlers, and pimps do not travel and they seldom, if ever, change personas; rather, they forever and only inhabit legible forms of black masculinity: the stereotypes. On the one hand, the ever-shifting personas of Jay Z, also known as S. Carter, Hova, Jigga, and others, and on the other hand, Jay Z's global savoir-faire, are descriptive details that Neal deploys in order to illustrate a "fracture" in hip hop's gender and sexuality problem.[21] Rather than simple flexing his thug muscles, throughout his musical career Jay Z's multiple and shifting personas effectively queers the restrictive identitarian lines of black gender and sexuality, and thus blurs the normative precincts of race, by performing an imperturbable form of self-possession even to the point of conspicuous self-branding.

Yet, if one works through the hip hop cosmopolitanism that begets the "radical rescripting" that Neal sees in Jay Z, one is left, once again, with a subject that is synonymous with the pleasures of humanist thought. Predicated on discursive representations of lack, the ground that gives rise to hip hop cosmopolitanism as exhibited by Jay Z is the violence produced by antiblackness, a world where blackness reveals the necessity to delink from humanist notions of black self-possession. In other words, Neal understands black masculinity as something that has not been exhausted at the level of identity, and therefore he fails to understand it as a profound problematization. Despite expanding the parameters of black gender and sexual identities, sexual violence is unaccounted for and unacknowledged; that is, the very thing that should become legible is the violence that is the assignation of blackness. While the phenomenon of hip hop cosmopolitanism is relatively new, it anchors itself to the liberal humanism of Man, in order to establish a logic of relationality that supposedly overcomes the hypermasculinity that is symptomatic of a disequilibrium within hip hop. Therefore, hip hop cosmopolitanism is not an ethical demand *for* black people, but simply is part of an a priori acknowledgment of their humanity.

---

[19] Neal, *Looking for Leroy*, 36 and 63.
[20] Neal, *Looking for Leroy*, 38.
[21] Neal, "NIGGA: The twenty-first-Century Theoretical Superhero," 562.

Overall, there are several problems with MAN's reclamation of a progressive black masculinity, perhaps the most fundamental of which is that it doubles down on the basic humanist paradigm that produces the biocentric construction of gender and sexual identities as antiblack, as a rule. Neal accepts the concept of gendered particularity without interrogating its debt to racial particularity and the universal Man for which both "race" and "gender" are merely genres of the master concept. Much of academic black feminism and hip hop feminism attempts to counter what it poses as the exclusionary practices of feminism and white supremacy by including black females within the privileges of gender.[22] In hip hop studies, this often means correcting the omission of black women and girls from the story of hip hop's development, critiquing misogynist sexual violence within hip hop, or exploring the unique vantage point expressed in women's performances. But the issue is *not* one of exclusion, but rather a *preclusion* constitutive to the structure of Western civilization.[23] Black feminism thus rests upon a faulty or underdeveloped diagnosis of the problem to be overcome. Blackness is not only the antithesis of whiteness, but it also signifies the position against which the human takes its form—and as such, blackness is also the negation of "manhood" and "womanhood," or in feminism's terms, of "gender" and "sex" themselves.[24] Wynter had signaled the tension inherent in these terms as long ago as the 1970s, followed by Hortense Spillers in the 1980s. In the 1990s, Saidiya Hartman extended their insights when she observed regarding slavery,

[22] See for example, Aria Halliday and Ashley N. Payne. "Introduction: Savage and savvy: Mapping contemporary hip hop feminism." *Journal of Hip Hop Studies* 7.1 (2020); Pyar J. Seth, "The First Time I Heard: Black Feminist Approaches to Hip Hop Methodologies." *Cultural Studies↔ Critical Methodologies* 23.5 (2023): 427–436; Karen Jaime, ""I'm A Stripper, Ho": The Sonics of Cardi B's Ratchet, Diasporic Feminism." *Performance Matters* 8.1 (2022): 83–96.

[23] See P. Khalil Saucier and Tryon P. Woods, "Ex Aqua: The Mediterranean Basin, Africans on the Move, and the Politics of Policing," *Theoria: A Journal of Social and Political Theory*, no. 141, December 2014: 55–75.

[24] See, for example, Sylvia Wynter, "One Love—Rhetoric or Reality? Aspects of Afro-Jamaicanism," *Caribbean Studies* 12, no 3 (1972): 64–97. For a superb overview of Wynter's contributions on this score, see Greg Thomas, "The Body Politics of 'Man' and 'Woman' in an 'Antiblack' World: Sylvia Wynter on Empire's Humanism (A Critical Resource Guide), in P. Khalil Saucier and Tryon P. Woods, eds., *On Maroonage: Ethical Confrontations with Antiblackness* (Trenton: Africa World Press, 2015).

that "[g]ender, if at all appropriate in this scenario, must be understood as indissociable from violence."[25]

The framework that Wynter, Spillers, and Hartman employ does not come from black feminism—and not because black feminism has claimed these theorists as its own while marginalizing or perverting their insights on this score (which it has also done). Instead, the font of knowledge is the black freedom struggle itself, and specifically the way black militancy has understood its confrontation with the particular modalities of tyranny that converge on the black body. The formulations emergent during the Black Power era are, for example, particularly instructive. In her classic Black Arts Movement-era anthology *The Black Woman*, Toni Cade Bambara proposed dispensing of "black woman" and "black man" in favor of "blackhood."[26] Similarly, Black Liberation Army soldier Safiya Bukhari wrote of her comrades in the movement, "We had taken on the persona of sexist America, but with a Black hue. It was into this context that the Black Panther Party was born, declaring that we were revolutionaries and a revolutionary had no gender."[27] These are the standards of leadership and analysis pertinent to the study of black expressive culture not to be found within the precincts of academic black feminism.

Neal's program of reclaiming gender and sexual sovereignty for black males and females is an example of what Wynter refers to as the overrepresentation of Man, literally and figuratively. Wynter writes that we must avoid "taking the ontological 'facts' of ethnicity (non-White and White) as well as of gender, sexuality, and culture, as if these were things-in-themselves, rather than 'totemic' signifiers in an overall system of resemblances and differences."[28] MAN's affirmation of a black feminist masculinity is more than aspirational. It attempts an inversion of a void, a reversal of a negation, for a people for whom gender differentiation as a principal marker of human standing has not only been forcibly denied, but moreover, this foreclosure continues to quarantine the freedom-seeking

[25] Saidiya V. Hartman, *Scenes of Seduction: Terror, Slavery, and Self-Making in Nineteenth-Century America* (New York: Oxford, 1997), 86.

[26] Toni Cade Bambara, ed., *The Black Woman: An Anthology* (New York: Washington Square Press, 2005).

[27] Safiya Bukhari, *The War Before* (New York: Feminist Press, 2010), 54–55.

[28] Sylvia Wynter, "On disenchanting discourse: 'minority' literary criticism and beyond." *Cultural Critique* 7 (1987): 217.

energies of contemporary black cultural expression.[29] In other words, it treats the world not as it is and has been for nearly a millennium, but rather as the upwardly mobile academic would like it to be. In this way, gender differentiation in black works much like a chokehold because it permits no adequate response. You cannot, under any circumstances, satisfactorily comply with the demand of the chokehold because it invariably provokes your resistance. As Jared Sexton explains, "We might even say that it imposes one's resistance upon oneself. Worse still, it then uses that resistance against itself, since the chokehold does not only persist to the extent that is resisted, it also tightens. One cannot comply and one cannot escape; there is no mediation or negotiation in this direct relation of force."[30] The reason why gender functions as a chokehold in this way is because its very purpose is to demand that black people prove their humanity by showing that they are not threats to public safety and sanctity. But blacks are construed as threatening in their very being, not for any particular conduct or performance. It is therefore as impossible for blacks to become legible as gendered subjects as it is for anyone to submit to the chokehold.[31]

READING VIOLENCE AND CREATIVITY: BONDS OF CONSPICUOUS CONSUMPTION

The violence of slavery produced gender differentiation that lives on as antiblackness in the modern world's monohumanist culture. A key social control purpose of gender is to disseminate an abridged conception of this ongoing violence. The tragic irony here is that black feminism's policing of black liberation has effectively obscured how, in Tommy Curry's words, the "sexual violence against Black men and boys has remained a routine, and historically denied, aspect of anti-Black racism."[32] In fact, Curry argues, the hegemony of black feminism in the multicultural academy has made such violence "unapproachable" theoretically, analytically, and in terms of educational praxis.[33] This sexual violence against black males

---

[29] Jared Sexton, *Black Men, Black Feminism: Lucifer's Nocturne* (Cham, Switzerland: Springer Nature, 2018), 32.

[30] Sexton, *Black Men,* 6.

[31] Sexton, *Black Men,* 6.

[32] Curry, *The Man-Not,* 143.

[33] Curry, *The Man-Not,* 143.

takes all the same forms as that experienced by females, including incest, rape, made-to-penetrate, domestic violence, intimate partner violence, harassment and assault in the workplace, and state violence. The *National Intimate Partner and Sexual Violence Survey* published by the Centers for Disease Control reveals that black males experience contact sexual violence as frequently as black females and endure higher rates of sexual victimization than white women.[34] The invisibility of sexual violence against black males is a component of the larger silence of male sexual victimization generally: studies show that males and females report similar rates of nonconsensual sex during a 12-month period.[35] Given the fact that males make up half of the population, it should not be surprising that they comprise roughly half of all victims of sexual violence—except that the prevailing raced and gendered constructs of both sex and violence make this reality opaque. Since power is the operative factor in sexual violence, not sexuality, and black males tend to be structurally disadvantaged relative to all non-blacks, it should also not be surprising that they are more sexually vulnerable than white women, as the higher rates of black male victimization affirm. Despite the copious quantities of ink expended to deconstruct the deeply sedimented racist mythology of the black male's sexual predations and the white female's vulnerability, the lore of white women's victimization at the hands of black men continues to effectively invert the reality.

This inversion of reality is not simply a nagging legacy of the Jim Crow era of lynching. Even though black feminism of the 1990s ostensibly called to task the racism of the second wave feminist movement, the conformity between white and black feminists when it comes to stereotypes of black male sexuality is uncanny. Susan Brownmiller notoriously claimed

[34] S. G. Smith, et al., The National Intimate Partner and Sexual Violence Survey (NISVS): 2010–2012 State Report (Atlanta, GA: National Center for Injury Prevention and Control, Centers for Disease Control and Prevention. 2017), Accessed May 10, 2024. https://www.cdc.gov/violenceprevention/pdf/NISVS-State ReportBook.pdf. See also, Tommy J. Curry E.A. Utley, "She Touched Me: Five Snapshots of Adult Sexual Violations of Black Boys," *Kennedy Institute of Ethics Journal* 28, 2 (2018): 205–241; Nathaniel Bryan, "Black Boys and Mental Health in Urban Communities" *The Palgrave Encyclopedia of Critical Perspectives on Mental Health*, (Cham: Springer International Publishing, 2022), 1–6.

[35] See Lara Stemple, Andrew Flores, and Ilan Meyer, "Sexual victimization perpetrated by women: Federal data reveal surprising prevalence," *Aggression and Violent Behavior* 34 (2017): 302–311; Lara Stemple and Ilan Meyer, "The sexual victimization of men in America: New data challenge old assumptions," *American Journal of Public Health* 104 (6) 2014: e19–e26.

that rape, especially gang rape, is a more normal, violent, and prevalent practice among black males than among their white counterparts. Brownmiller opined that sexual violence was a normal feature of the black male's subculture of violence as a way for them to project their manhood in the aftermath of Jim Crow segregation.[36] Black feminists have excoriated Brownmiller in their indictment of racism in the women's movement.[37] As Curry points out, however, doyenne of third wave feminism bell hooks echoed Brownmiller's assertion that black males are more violent, maintaining that they take pleasure in their violence and the fear it cultivates in others. In her 2004 book *We Real Cool: Black Men and Masculinity*, hooks states, "Overall, the facts reveal that black males are more violent than ever before in this nation."[38]

The spectacle of police killings, combined with the perceived threat of hypermasculinity within and beyond hip hop, conjoins to obscure and mystify the "sexualized police violence" that confronts black men and boys, such as with Manning's assault at the hands of Philadelphia police cited earlier. As the Manning case and many others illustrate, black males suffer from sexual violence both in the past and present times, beyond the fatalism documented by the likes of Victor Rios, Sudhir Venkatesh, and Alfred Young, Jr. As connoted in the title of Young's book, *Are Black Men Doomed?*, this brand of quasi-social science pop-journalism asserts that the accumulated effect of racial stereotyping, abandonment, and interpersonal violence is that black males are an "endangered species."[39] The unexamined acceptance of gender differentiation in black masks the thinly veiled assumption that black males are properly categorized within the animal kingdom, below human beings. Hip hop has accentuated a depoliticized interpretation of the interpersonal violence of the street, and hip hop studies has followed suit in ignoring the robust breadth of sexual violence in which black male victimization unfolds. Hip hop studies and its form of black feminism is thus complicit in fortifying Western slaveholding culture's genres of gender and its original fetish object, the black body. It has

---

[36] Susan Brownmiller, *Against Our Will: Men, Women, and Rape* (New York: Fawcett, 1975), 174–209.

[37] See Angela Y. Davis, *Women, Race, and Class* (New York: Vintage, 1983).

[38] hooks, *We Real Cool*, 52.

[39] Victor M. Rios, *Punished: Policing the lives of Black and Latino boys* (New York: NYU Press, 2011); Sudhir A. Venkatesh, *Off the books: The underground economy of the urban poor*, (Cambridge, MA: Harvard University Press, 2006); Alford A. Young Jr., *Are Black men doomed?* (New York: John Wiley & Sons, 2018).

played a significant role in reproducing the black body as "a hungered-after taboo item and a nightmarish bugbear in the badlands of the American racial imagination."[40]

In this context, "GOMD" creates an intervention against the hyperbole of toxic masculinity and the "undervaluation" of sexual offenses against all black people.[41] The video for "GOMD" is a typical plantation scene, with slaves toiling in the house and in the field, and whites reveling in their sadistic status of mastery. There are tensions between the house and the field slaves, recalling Malcolm X's famous allegory from his "Message to the Grassroots" speech. J. Cole's character in the video is the head house slave and thus draws the antipathy of all the slaves. He turns this disunity on its head, however, by stealing the keys to the master's armory and passing out the weapons to the field slaves. Rebellion ensues, resulting in the whites being tied up, the plantation aflame, and Africans dancing around a bonfire fueled by furniture from the master's house. Hip hop studies views the video as portraying black agency, a visual explication of liberty and freedom, of the masses seizing the moment to establish an equal footing, both intraracially and interracially. Overcoming the disunity within blackness rehearses a common theme across black culture, the tension between collective revolt and individual gain. The refrain of "GOMD" is cathartic; one could imagine the forceful cry to "get off my dick" as a declaration of self-defense and bodily integrity in the barracoon, the schooner, the plantation, prison cell, police car, classroom, workplace, and beyond, all highly eroticized and violent spaces.

A more material reading of power, however, limns the exultation of freedom song. The video and song lyrics allow us to discuss the suspension of temporality, the time-space gap that connects the plantation with the contemporary governance of antiblackness. J. Cole's refrain directs us to make these connections; it is *not* freedom, in other words, but an utterance, a shout out against what is. If we hear "GOMD" this way, it can direct us to a more ethical assessment of life under humanism's antiblack protocols, illuminating avenues of fugitivity and marronage along the way. "GOMD" opens the doors to access the unspeakable. As Thomas Foster notes, the sexual violation of black males "dangerously points out cracks

[40] Greg Tate, *Everything but the burden: What White people are taking from Black culture* (New York: Crown, 2003), 4.

[41] Shelby Mitchell, "The Societal and Prosecutorial Undervaluation of Sexual Offenses Against Black Men," *Rutgers Race & Law Review*, 23 (2021): 479.

in the marble base of patriarchy that asserts men as penetrators in opposition to the penetrable."[42] J. Cole, intentionally or unwittingly, demonstrates one way of representing the sexual objectification of blackness, of the black body as "an energy source" for Man and its genres of gender differentiation.[43] A comparative study found that young black males experienced statutory rape, sexual coercion, and sexual manipulation more than any other group.[44] Although both black male and female children are particularly at risk for abuse compared with white children, black boys are more likely to be victims of actual or attempted sexual intercourse.[45] Unsurprisingly, this trauma is linked to depression, increased risk-taking, and increased chances of intimate partner violence perpetration and victimization later in these boys' lives.[46]

Although violence by black males, actual and symbolic, is virtually never conceived in relation to this reality of prior sexual victimization in their lives, "this oversight is a scandal for critical thought given the ubiquity of antiblack sexual violence" across the eras.[47] Black culture itself has found it difficult to represent this trauma in anything other than circumscribed terms. Toni Morrison's chain-gang scene in her novel *Beloved* obliquely references white-on-black male rape in a manner that registers the silence surrounding this violence.[48] But the preponderance of this trauma means that "it is imperative that critical analysis behold hip hop culture writ large as embodying this context of sexual violence."[49] MAN grossly under

---

[42] Thomas Foster, "The sexual abuse of Black men under American slavery," *Journal of the History of Sexuality* 20.3 (2011): 448.

[43] Vincent Woodard, *The Delectable Negro: Human Consumption and Homoeroticism within US Slave Culture* (New York: NYU University Press), 14.

[44] See for example, B.H. French, J. Tilghman, and D. Malebranche, "Sexual coercion context and psychosocial correlates among diverse males," *Psychology of Men and Masculinity*, 16, 1 (2015): 42–53.

[45] See J.T. Hernandez., M. Lodico, and R.J. DiClemente, "The effects of child abuse and race on risk taking in male adolescence. *Journal of the National Medical Association*, 85, 5 (1993): 593–597.

[46] See Tommy J. Curry, and Ebony A. Utley. "She touched me: Five snapshots of adult sexual violations of black boys."

[47] Woods, *Blackhood*, 202.

[48] Toni Morrison, *Beloved* (New York: Vintage, 2004), 107–108. For the historical record on this sexual violence, see for example Sharon Block, *Rape and sexual power in early America*. UNC Press Books, 2006; Thomas A. Foster, *Rethinking Rufus: Sexual Violations of Enslaved Men* (Athens: University of Georgia Press, 2019).

[49] Woods, *Blackhood*, 203.

appreciates the salience of this context for interpreting popular culture because he fails to ascertain how "[w]ithin the contested field of representation and counternarratives of black performance, racialized policing and punishment emerges simultaneously with a traumatic sexual violence that constitutes an effaced engagement with the history of plantation slavery and its production of modes of black selfhood, its desires, and practices."[50] Since hip hop masculinities are seen as always and already preoccupied with their erasure—"emasculation"—calibrating our reading practices to elucidate this terrain is key to not contribute to its further silencing.

"GOMD" is thus the eerie echo haunting the archive, which remains as unspeakable in black culture today as it was in the life interviews conducted with ex-slaves in the early twentieth century by the Works Project Administration. While the black feminism of hip hop studies would see "GOMD" as an expression of hypermasculinity and heteronormative patriarchy in black, we suggest such a reading truncates the context of its utterance and problematically extends the biocentrism of race and gender identity designed to occlude the sexual violence constitutive to our contemporary order. Instead, we suggest that "GOMD" is a window into how "the inability to creatively imagine homosexuality during slavery reflected a fundamental fear within the black collective of moving outside of the normative categories of masculinity, reproduction, pleasure, and family."[51] The "sexual/libidinal appetite for African flesh" persists, with the ubiquitous stop-and-frisk police encounter and the hip hop video as but two widespread examples of "black consumption."[52] In every instance, the police encounter affirms the intrinsic sexual assault embedded within Fourth Amendment search and seizure. "Reasonable suspicion," as both legal and discursive assault, therefore, is sexual violence, innately, and today is deployed to consume blackness in order to establish the gender identity of the human.[53] In a routine stop-and-frisk, to use Vincent Woodard's description, "[t]he African body is spread-eagled before this tableau of male bonding."[54] J. Cole's video thus merges time, past and present, despite the perception that the lyrics do not fit with the plantation scene depicted in the video. They do fit the antiblack logic of the world

[50] Woods, *Blackhood*, 203.
[51] Woodard, *The Delectable Negro*, 22.
[52] Woodard, *The Delectable Negro*, 10.
[53] Woods, *Blackhood*, 173.
[54] Woodard, *The Delectable Negro*, 10.

which normalizes exploitative and violent social relations by naturalizing white agency and black dispossession regardless of gender. The video allows for a synchronic exploration of black sexual violence. As if channeling the ancestors, J. Cole could be speaking to a perpetrator today, or from the past, intimating how culture is inscribed in the body. Within the literal hold of the slave ship, gender difference becomes lost as Africans become black; as the slave ships traverse the oceans, replacing one cultural context with another, the black body becomes unmade and converted into an object of desire and consumption for Man. This violence was enacted equally upon all Africans, male and female alike, positioning all blacks within what Angela Davis has termed "the deformed equality of equal oppression," and leading Spillers to argue that antiblackness ungenders black people. "Get off my dick," then, is not an anatomical reference, nor an expression of gendered self-possession, but rather a reference to the fact of antiblack sexual violence against males and females alike that is constitutive to the modern world. "Get off my dick" is thus an exhortation for female self-defense as much as it is for male: it is the collective that is violated, not the gendered individual of the monohumanist imagination.[55]

READING PERFORMATIVITY: MAN's THRESHOLD

Cultural politics must be calibrated to an antiblack world, for antiblackness constitutes the world and is not a mere moment in time that fades with Emancipation, civil rights legislation, or the discrediting of white supremacy. Despite this context, culture is often perceived as an escape or a mode of resistance. Culture imagines and produces resistance, too, but this aspirational mode of reading hip hop tends to crowd out the kind of reading we advance here of a synchronic and diagnostic analysis of power. As a spectacle of resistance (which is how hip hop is reductively perceived generally), "GOMD" is seductive for those like MAN and the black feminist hip hop scholars who work from within the liberal humanism of Man. We might call this a politics of remediation for Man-in-black—alternative to this approach, we offer a reading of cultural practice that underscores the limits of performativity.

[55] For a similar reading of Lil' Kim along these lines, see Greg Thomas, *Hip-Hop Revolution in the Flesh: Power, Knowledge, and Pleasure in Lil' Kim's Lyricism* (New York: Palgrave Macmillan, 2009).

The first impression is that the video and lyrics for "GOMD" do not seem to go together. However, if we take seriously racial slavery beyond the historiographical, and understand the socialization of slavery, then the lyrical and visual bridge time and space and call into question our assumption that existence unfolds in a linear fashion.[56] In a post on his blog several years ago, through ideas ultimately fleshed out in his book *Looking for Leroy: Illegible Masculinities* and elsewhere, Neal found political significance in the video for "GOMD." He describes the video in terms of "When 'Thingness' Stages the Terms of Their Freedom":

> If we are to think of chattel slavery as the attempt to reduce Black humanity to a "Thingness," what happens when that Thingness (pre-citizen in the eyes of the law) stages the terms of its own freedom, using the very thingness (culture and commodities) that it created but can never own, because Thingness can't own thingness, let alone itself?[57]

For Neal, J. Cole and video director Lawrence Lamont stage this black resistance-as-criminality, and in so doing, remind us that hip hop has consistently re-staged "the terms of our resistance."

Although Neal's comments on "GOMD" are brief, they distill not only his general approach to hip hop studies, but the leading disposition of the field as a whole: that hip hop "stages the terms" of black freedom. We argue that this sentiment is always and already incomplete if decoupled from the reality that such freedom moves can never extend beyond mere staging: hip hop studies' emphasis on the performative dimension of oppression and resistance, at the expense of diligently analyzing power as a structure, does a disservice to the actual protracted work of building toward black liberation. We disagree with Neal's assessment about "GOMD." When reading the song lyrics together with the images of the video, we see J. Cole as offering a wake-up call, for black people to get clear about their roots, cut through the bullshit existence in materialist white supremacist society, and remember that if life is to have a future it must be grounded in reciprocity and collective struggle (with the end of

---

[56] On the socialization of slavery, see Tryon P. Woods, "Slavery and the U.S. Prison System," *Global Policy*, May 6, 2021, Accessed June 1, 2024. https://www.globalpolicy-journal.com/blog/06/05/2021/slavery-and-us-prison-system

[57] Neal, Mark Anthony, "*When "Thingness" Stages the Terms of Their Freedom: J. Cole's "G.O.M.D."* New Black Man, March 24, 2015, Accessed June 5, 2024. http://newblack-man.blogspot.com/2015/03/when-thingness-stages-terms-of-their.html

the video illustrating this key point). While there is much more to say on this account, for economy's sake we will focus on that dimension of fugitivity that consumes Neal's attention. According to Neal, hip hop stages black resistance "via its sampling practices (Thingness stealing thingness)…using the very thingness (culture and commodities) that it created but can never own." The issue of sampling practices generates glaring discrepancies in how the two very different creative acts of performance and rebellion are imagined. To drive home this point, Jim Vernon's *Sampling, Biting, and the Postmodern Subversion of Hip Hop* illustrates the fabulation of subversion that has been circulated and infinitely repeated by many hip hop studies scholars at the expense of an accurate analysis of power. Vernon rightfully suggests that if we take hip hop culture seriously, the fifth element of hip hop, "knowledge," is in direct confrontation with the so-called culture of rebellion "affirmed by the 'subversive' reactionary postmodernist strain of Hip Hop Studies" which valorizes self-possession.[58] That is to say, hip hop scholars have routinely imposed contrary (and by extension, detached) regimes of knowledge or interpretative value systems over a sincere heretical cultural movement.[59] In this case, Neal is referring to the slaves' theft of the implements of rebellion from the slave master, a stealing of "thingness" to liberate "thingness" that corresponds to J. Cole's sampling of "Berta, Berta" from playwright August Wilson's 1987 play *The Piano Lesson*, a recording of which Branford Marsalis included on his 1992 Grammy Award-winning blues-tribute album *I Heard You Twice The First Time*.

Closer examination of J. Cole's culling of "Berta, Berta" produces, for us, a different inflection on black performance than that found by Neal. Wilson featured the prison work song in a scene wherein the characters recall time spent at the Mississippi State Penitentiary, the notorious Parchman Farm. The song's performance in the play, set in 1936 Pittsburgh, extends the captivity of Parchman, already an extension of the slave plantation into post-Emancipation time, into the urban spaces of the North to which blacks migrated as a form of self-defense in hopes of escaping racial violence. Wilson's play thus references blues culture's emergence as the language of liberation's crushing deferral. The singing of "Berta,

---

[58] Jim Vernon, *Sampling, biting, and the postmodern subversion of hip hop* (Cham, Switzerland; Palgrave Macmillan, 2021).

[59] See for example, Arnett Powell and Adebayo Olorunto (also known as Nightjohn), *The Hiphop Driven Life: A Genius Liberation Handbook* (Baltimore: Afrikan World Books, 2005).

Berta" does not stage the characters' liberation; on the contrary, it signifies their ongoing captivity and how they reckon with its terms. As Wilson expressed in his 1982 play *Ma Rainey's Black Bottom*, "White folks don't understand about the blues. They hear it come out but they don't know how it got there. They don't understand that's life's way of talking. You don't sing to feel better. You sing 'cause that's a way of understanding life." The performance of the prison work song in *The Piano Lesson*, therefore, does more than simply recall past experiences in the black characters' lives; it signifies how the past continues to live in the present, including how they enter the conflict at the center of *The Piano Lesson*: Boy Willie's desire to sell the family piano, and his sister Berniece's adamant refusal to allow it to be sold.

The piano represents the ongoing slave relations constituting black existence well into the twentieth century. The white man who owned Boy Willie and Berniece's family paid for the purchase of the piano by breaking up another slave family by selling mother and child—black slaves as real estate. The white man obtained the piano as a gift for his wife, but the wife missed the slaves who were exchanged for the instrument, so that family's father, who was a skilled carpenter, was ordered to carve the likenesses of the mother and child into the sides of the piano. Boy Willie and Berniece's father eventually stole the piano in 1911 from his former master, a transgression for which he was killed. Berniece's mother would mourn the loss of her husband by incessantly polishing the piano and having Berniece play on it for her. After her mother's death, Berniece shut the piano, never to play it again out of fear that it would disturb the ghosts of her ancestors. She believes that she is protecting her own daughter from this painful past by not playing the piano any longer. Meanwhile, the ghost of the former slave master can be seen playing on the piano in Berniece's house, and Boy Willie conspires to sell the piano to purchase the land on which the family was formerly enslaved.

Wilson's play stands as a treatise on how slavery produces property and real estate in relation to culture and against the "relations" of blackness that the culture of property simultaneously finds and destroys, perpetually reiterated across time and space. Wilson's dramatic rendering of this process highlights the violence carved into the grains of the piano and lilting into the choked atmosphere of its performances. More importantly for our aim to understand "GOMD," the performances of Wilson's plays are part of a blues tradition in which there is no pretense to freedom or to transcending the violence of the surround. At best, there is only fugitivity, a dogged perseverance of readying for liberation while dealing with the mundane day-to-day struggles of the antiblack world. As a cipher for life, then, the blues deals squarely with the world as it is while living to see a new day. Nobody ever suggests that the blues "stage the terms of its own freedom." Instead, it is widely recognized as a sober assessment of the pain, violence, and cost of being black in a world made in slavery's image. But such a confrontation, likewise, is regarded as requisite for freedom and not as submission, defeat, or acquiescence. In the early twenty-first century, we seem to believe that the blues is no longer applicable, that we have transcended the travails necessitating a blues witnessing, leaving us with performances of triumph and freedom realized. Likewise, for some reason, representations of pain are today seen as defeatist.

Neal's reading of J. Cole's performance of resistance flaunts the blues tradition from which hip hop descends and to which "GOMD" specifically refers. Additionally, Neal's reading rests on the mythic reality of freedom in property's appropriation implied by his notion of "thingness stealing thingness." Why does "GOMD" signify the staging of freedom and not the ongoing suffering of captivity? Such assurance in the face of the preponderance of evidence to the contrary mystifies not only the actual black struggle, protracted across the generations, but it more alarmingly must contort the very historical cues laced into the song through the sampling that Neal celebrates as hip hop's "thingness stealing thingness." When we factor in the song's title and its chorus, "get off my dick," the real world of antiblack sexual violence opens up to us in ways that Neal forecloses. As noted earlier, "get off my dick" uttered in hip hop fashion connotes contemporary stop-and-frisk policing and so much more in terms of persistent scenes of black sexual trauma, while its overlay on scenes of the pastoral South conjures up lynching in the post-Emancipation period and the regime of sexual assault yoking antebellum slavery to the century of Jim Crow. As Wynter, Spillers, and Hartman observe, gender dissembles in the face of such violence against both male and female enslaved Africans, contra the feminization of slavery's sexual violence in much of "black feminism."[60] Moreover, we can read "get off my dick" as

---

[60] See also, Carole Boyce Davies, "Con-di-fi-cation: Transnationalism, diaspora and the limits of domestic racial or feminist discourses." *JENdA: A Journal of Culture and African Women Studies* 9 (2006): 1–39; Greg Thomas, "PROUD FLESH Inter/Views: Elaine Brown." *ProudFlesh: New Afrikan Journal of Culture, Politics and Consciousness* 1.2 (2003): 1–14.

J. Cole staying many steps ahead of hip hop studies in his exposure of how black men continue to suffer through sexual violence—including, not to mention, how such violence is staged through the popular culture industries of hip hop. This is not a performance of freedom, in other words, but a blues prosecution of its violent deferral.

More than anything, "GOMD" becomes an instructive and pedagogical popular culture artifact, a testimony about how the black body remains ensnared within the logics of racial slavery, long after the institution's formal demise. MAN fails to recognize a different kind of capacity to act, one which is made possible through the aesthetic yet is developed in close analysis of the composition and effect of structural forces. J. Cole's "GOMD," on the other hand, is a blues critique in which the aesthetic is reflective of the world's antiblack structures. At its best, this what hip hop can do; when it is ethical, hip hop studies amplifies this critique. Unfortunately, much of hip hop studies is not critique at all, but simply an expression of identity wherein the possessive individual of Western monohumanism is vivified at the expense of an accurate analysis of power in the world in which we must live.

BIBLIOGRAPHY

The Associated Press, "Officer accused of rupturing teen's testicle during search," *NBC 10*, January 18, 2014. Accessed May 1, 2024. https://www.nbcphiladelphia.com/news/national-international/officer-accused-of-rupturing-teens-testicle-during-search/85663/

Bambara, Toni Cade, ed., *The Black Woman: An Anthology*. New York: Washington Square Press, 2005.

Block, Sharon. *Rape and sexual power in early America*. Chapel Hill: University of North Carolina Press, 2006.

Bradley, Regina N. "Re-imagining slavery in the hiP-hoP imagination." *South: a scholarly journal* 49.1 (2016): 3-24.

Brownmiller, Susan. *Against our will: Men, women, and rape*. New York: Ballantine Books, 1993.

Bryan, Nathaniel. "Black Boys and Mental Health in Urban Communities." In *The Palgrave Encyclopedia of Critical Perspectives on Mental Health*, 1-6. Cham: Springer International Publishing, 2022.

Bukhari, Safiya. *The War Before: The True Life Story of Becoming a Black Panther, Keeping the Faith in Prison, and Fighting for Those Left Behind*. New York: Feminist Press, 2010.

Chilburn, Eric. "Black Men Participating in College Sports May Be More Vulnerable to Sexual Abuse," *Insight Into Higher Ed*, March 16, 2022. Accessed May 1, 2024.https://www.insightintodiversity.com/black-men-participating-in-college-sports-may-be-more-vulnerable-to-sexual-abuse/

Curry, Tommy J. *The Man-Not: Race, Class and Genre and the Dilemmas of Black Manhood*. Philadelphia: Temple University Press, 2017.

Curry, Tommy J., and Ebony A. Utley. "She touched me: Five snapshots of adult sexual violations of black boys." *Kennedy institute of ethics journal* 28, no. 2 (2018): 205-241.

Davis, Angela Y. *Women, Race & Class*. New York: Vintage, 1983.

Davies, Carole Boyce. "Con-di-fi-cation: Transnationalism, diaspora and the limits of domestic racial or feminist discourses." *JENdA: A Journal of Culture and African Women Studies* 9 (2006): 1-39.

Ferreira da Silva, Denise., "Sending Language into Battle: Interview with Hortense J. Spillers." *boundary 2* 51, no. 1 (2024): 3-37.

Foster, Thomas. "The sexual abuse of Black men under American slavery." *Journal of the History of Sexuality* 20, no. 3 (2011): 445-464.

———. *Rethinking Rufus: Sexual Violations of Enslaved Men*. Vol. 2. Athens: University of Georgia Press, 2019.

French, B. H., Tilghman, J., & Malebranche, D. "Sexual coercion context and psychosocial correlates among diverse males." *Psychology of Men and Masculinity*, 16, 1 (2015): 42–53.

Halliday, Aria S. and Payne, Ashley N. "Introduction: Savage and Savvy: Mapping Contemporary Hip Hop Feminism." *Journal of Hip Hop Studies*. Vol. 7: Iss. 1, Article 3 (2020). Available at: https://scholarscompass.vcu.edu/jhhs/vol7/iss1/3

Hartman, Saidiya V. *Scenes of Seduction: Terror, Slavery, and Self-Making in Nineteenth-Century America*. New York: Oxford, 1997.

Hernandez, Jeanne T., Mark Lodico, and Ralph J. DiClemente. "The effects of child abuse and race on risk-taking in male adolescents." *Journal of the National Medical Association* 85, no. 8 (1993): 593–597.

Hill Collins, Patricia *Black Sexual Politics: African Americans, Gender, and the New Racism*. New York: Routledge, 2004.

hooks, bell. *We Real Cool: Black Men and Masculinity*. New York: Routledge, 2004.

J. Cole. *2014 Forest Hills Drive*. 2014. Columbia.

Jaime, Karen. ""I'm A Stripper, Ho": The Sonics of Cardi B's Ratchet, Diasporic Feminism." *Performance Matters* 8.1 (2022): 83-96.

Loevy and Loevy, "Milwaukee Settles Racially Tinged Cavity Strip Search Suit," *Loevy.com*, January 19, 2016. Accessed May 1, 2024. https://www.loevy.com/milwaukee-settles-racially-tinged-body-cavity-strip-search-suit-with-74-black-men/

McKittrick, Katherine, ed. *Sylvia Wynter: On being human as praxis.* Duke University Press, 2015.

Miller, Larry, "Officer cleared in Darrin Manning Investigation, *The Philadelphia Tribune,* July 17, 2014. Accessed May 1, 2024. https://www.phillytrib.com/news/officer-cleared-in-darrin-manning-investigation/article_7868b987-b3ee-5a6c-a9e5-ee8f6219df91.html

Mitchell, S. "The Societal and Prosecutorial Undervaluation of Sexual Offenses Against Black Men." *Rutgers Race & Law Review.,* 23, (2021).

Morrison, Toni. *Beloved.* New York: Vintage Books, 2004.

Neal, Mark Anthony. *Looking for Leroy: Illegible Black Masculinities.* New York: New York University Press, 2013a.

———. "NIGGA: The 21st-Century Theoretical Superhero." *Cultural Anthropology* 28.3 (2013b): 557-58.

———. "When "Thingness" Stages the Terms of Their Freedom: J. Cole's "G.O.M.D." *New Black Man,* March 24, 2015. Accessed June 5, 2024. http://newblackman.blogspot.com/2015/03/when-thingness-stages-terms-of-their.html

Powell, Arnett and Adebayo Olorunto (also known as Nightjohn). *The Hiphop Driven Life: A Genius Liberation Handbook.* Baltimore: Afrikan World Books, 2005.

Rios, Victor M. *Punished: Policing the lives of Black and Latino boys.* New York: NYU Press, 2011

Saucier, P. Khalil, and Tryon P. Woods. "Ex aqua: The Mediterranean basin, Africans on the move, and the politics of policing." *Theoria* 61, no. 141 (2014): 55-75.

Seth, Pyar J. "The First Time I Heard: Black Feminist Approaches to Hip Hop Methodologies." *Cultural Studies↔ Critical Methodologies* 23.5 (2023): 427-436.

Sexton, Jared. *Black Men, Black Feminism: Lucifer's Nocturne.* Cham, Switzerland: Springer Nature, 2018.

Smith, S.G. et al., The National Intimate Partner and Sexual Violence Survey (NISVS): 2010–2012 State Report (Atlanta, GA: National Center for Injury Prevention and Control, Centers for Disease Control and Prevention. 2017). Accessed May 10, 2024. https://www.cdc.gov/violenceprevention/pdf/NISVS-State ReportBook.pdf.

Stemple, Lara, and Ilan H. Meyer. "The sexual victimization of men in America: New data challenge old assumptions." *American journal of public health* 104, no. 6 (2014): e19-e26.

Stemple, Lara, Andrew Flores, and Ilan H. Meyer. "Sexual victimization perpetrated by women: Federal data reveal surprising prevalence." *Aggression and violent behavior* 34 (2017): 302-311.

Tate, Greg. *Everything but the burden: What White people are taking from Black culture.* New York: Crown, 2003.

Thomas, Greg. "PROUD FLESH Inter/Views: Elaine Brown." *ProudFlesh: New Afrikan Journal of Culture, Politics and Consciousness* 1.2 (2003): 1-14.
———. *Hip-Hop Revolution in the Flesh: Power, Knowledge, and Pleasure in Lil' Kim's Lyricism*. New York: Palgrave Macmillan, 2009.
———. "The Body Politics of 'Man' and 'Woman' in an 'Antiblack' World: Sylvia Wynter on Empire's Humanism (A Critical Resource Guide)." In P. Khalil Saucier and Tryon P. Woods, eds., *On Maroonage: Ethical Confrontations with Antiblackness*. Trenton: Africa World Press, 2015.
Venkatesh, Sudhir Alladi. *Off the books: The underground economy of the urban poor*. Cambridge, MA: Harvard University Press, 2006.
Vernon, Jim. *Sampling, biting, and the postmodern subversion of hip hop*. Cham, Switzerland; Palgrave Macmillan, 2021.
Woodard, Vincent. *The Delectable Negro: Human Consumption and Homoeroticism within US Slave Culture*. New York: NYU University Press, 2014.
Woods, Tryon P. *Blackhood Against the Police Power: Punishment and Disavowal in the "Post-Racial" Era*. East Lansing: Michigan State, 2019.
———. "Slavery and the U.S. Prison System," *Global Policy*, May 6, 2021. Accessed June 1, 2024. https://www.globalpolicyjournal.com/blog/06/05/2021/slavery-and-us-prison-system.
Wynter, Sylvia. "One Love—Rhetoric or Reality? Aspects of Afro-Jamaicanism." *Caribbean Studies* 12, no 3 (1972): 64-97.
———. "On disenchanting discourse:" minority" literary criticism and beyond." *Cultural Critique* 7 (1987): 207-244.
Younge, Gary, "If Darrin Manning were a high school dropout, he'd still have the right to walk the streets unmolested, "*The Guardian*, January 27, 2014. Accessed May 1, 2024.https://www.theguardian.com/commentisfree/2014/jan/27/darrin-manning-high-school-deserving-victims
Young Jr, Alford A. *Are Black men doomed?*. New York: John Wiley & Sons, 2018.

INDEX[1]

[1] Note: Page numbers followed by 'n' refer to notes.

P. K. Saucier (ed.), *Critical Essays on Hip Hop and the Study of Hip Hop*, https://doi.org/10.1007/978-3-031-80763-3

The manufacturer's authorised representative in the EU is Springer
Nature Customer Service Centre GmbH, Europaplatz 3, 69115 Heidelberg,
Germany. If you have any concerns regarding our products, please
contact ProductSafety@springernature.com

Printed and bound by CPI Group (UK) Ltd, Croydon, CR0 4YY

24/04/2026

02096315-0013